JOURNEY OF THE SEED

CATCH THE BIBLE'S
BIG PICTURE
IN 60 DAYS

JEFF ANDERSON

Journey of The Seed

Catch the Bible's Big Picture in 60 Days

Copyright © 2019 Jeff Anderson

www.JeffAndersonAuthor.com
www.PowerReadTheBible.com

TABLE OF CONTENTS

INTRODUCTION………………………………………………..7

READING PLAN AND HELPFUL TOOLS …………… 23

DAILY SUMMARIES……………………………..………..29

TIMELINE CALCULATIONS………..…………….. 153

ABOUT JEFF ANDERSON ……………………………159

INTRODUCTION

The famous unread book

The Bible is the most famous book in history. It's not only the world's all time best seller, but it continues to be each year's best selling book year after year after year.

Ironically the Bible is a mostly unread book. Many people have Bibles in their homes and on their phones. But most don't read them.

For many children growing up in Christian households, when they leave home for college or to begin their adult lives they don't really know the Bible's central theme.

But it's not all their fault. Christian adults struggle with reading and grasping the Bible as well.

And there we have it - a recipe for full-on, widespread Biblical illiteracy. Parents and adults - that don't understand the Bible's big picture - are passing off the "knowledge baton" to children and teens in Christian homes and churches.

As expected, these second generation recipients are worse off than the ones before.

So what happens to these biblically illiterate souls?

It's a sad process.

Biblically deficient minds lead to dormant faith. And dormant faith often turns... faithless.

Tragic!

Megatrends of the Church

In 2010 George Barna released a report of the Top 6 megatrends affecting the church. The #1 trend – the Christian church is becoming less theologically literate. Biblical literacy is on the decline, Barna predicted. And that's exactly what has happened over the past decade.

Study after study affirms that young people from Christian homes are drifting away from the faith. And for those hanging on, many remain disillusioned and stunted in their growth and mostly detached from the Bible.

Lets get serious

We need to get serious about understanding and passing along truth in our families.

We need to discover a renewed sense of interest in opening God's word.

We need to ignite a new hunger for knowledge and to pursue the wisdom of God.

The current methods are failing. What we're doing is not working for our youth. And it's not working for adults either.

In general, parents are very interested in their children's success. We invest in soccer, baseball, piano and dance...and then college prep courses.

But when it comes to passing on biblical knowledge, we're far too casual. We've set the bar far too low.

Parents, it's time to declare war on our lackadaisical approach to the Bible. We must be in this book daily.

Church leaders, we must get serious. Let's not treat the Bible as a smorgasbord buffet (*Gee, I wonder what we'll serve them this week?*)

And if you're a teenager or young adult, this challenge is for you, too! Don't settle for ignorance about your faith.

We need to back up the truck to the knowledge station and start from the beginning. We need to process the full Bible.

What is the Bible about? What is God's story? What is the framework of understanding we need on which to build a lifetime of Bible reading?

What is the Bible's big picture?

Nursery Rhyme Faith

Many young Christians today suffer from what I call "nursery rhyme faith." We've given them simplistic platitudes, applauded when they parrot them back to us, and then wonder why their faith fades in high school or college.

"Jesus died on the cross for my sins", they say.

Yes, this truth is a powerful force in the heart of a child. The words might even help them want to be baptized. But the point is not getting kids baptized at eight years old. The goal is that they walk with God when they're eighteen and twenty-eight years old.

Where we've gone wrong

Your fourteen-year-old son goes off for summer camp. Forced to leave his cell phone home, he endures a week of spiritual bliss. Scheduled quiet times, Bible sessions, fire-side chats, praise and worship. On the final night your son walks down front with a host of peers. Upon return home he is baptized. But five years later he's questioning and abandoning his faith.

How is this happening?

One reason – we've not equipped them to grow in the full knowledge of God. Instead we trick them into an emotional experience and send them back home to nibble on an appetizer menu of select Bible pieces.

A little here, a little there. Some random scripture memory and targeted deep dive Bible study – usually a New Testament book with a focus on rules of living.

Live like this. Don't live like that. Don't have sex before marriage, avoid alcohol, don't gossip. You know, the basics.

Meanwhile they have no clue about the history or big picture of the faith.

We tell them to love like Jesus. But we don't tell them who Jesus really is or how he arrived at Bethlehem in the first place.

Stories and Myths

Over a lifetime in church, kids hear plenty of stories (those happy animals prancing into the ark, for example). After a while, these stories seem less impressive... and less believable. (*Were Adam and Eve even real?*)

They may try to hold on to "Jesus died on the cross," but if that's all they have the expression has less meaning for their life.

Faith is like a muscle. It must be exercised to become stronger.

There's a progression that builds on the fundamentals.

Think of how kids grow in mathematics. They start with addition and subtraction, then long division, and fractions. Later comes algebra, geometry, calculus.

They move from memorization to working out problems.

The same applies to reading and writing. After kids learn to copy the alphabet, they write words, then sentences, then paragraphs, then essays, and then thought-provoking research papers.

They move from imitation to articulation.

Meanwhile at church, it's *Jesus died on the cross for me*. And maybe singing some emotional praise songs in a dark room. Meanwhile young people are never challenged to ponder the deeper themes of the Christian faith.

Will God really judge mankind? Why did Jesus have to die? What kind of life will we live in heaven? How should Christians respond to social issues? Why do bad things happen to good people? Is hell even real?

The next thing they know, they're not really sure what they believe. And more importantly, they're not really sure it matters. *Faith isn't concrete, after all. A vague feeling is all we can expect, right?*

Young atheists and agnostics

Some of these adolescents grow up and cease to believe in God completely (atheism). What little faith structure they once held becomes swept away by ignorance and rejecting the truth.

Some aren't ready to fully disbelieve – so they settle for something more subtle. "We can't truly know for sure," they say. So they casually call themselves "agnostics."

The childlike faith they claimed as kids gives way to unanswered questions, then doubts, and then casual dismissal of the book (Bible) they failed to understand.

A few decades ago, the claim of agnosticism would send chills up a parent's spine. Today parents admit it casually ("Yeah, my grown child says they're basically agnostic.")

Adults are struggling too

I set out to address this problem of biblical ignorance among our young people.

But I quickly learned something revealing. Our adults are struggling too. They also lack basic biblical knowledge.

They know all the catchphrases and sound bite messages, just like their children. And just like their kids, they too were never encouraged to grow in the knowledge of God.

I started sponsoring Bible reading plans – helping parents and youth read through the entire Bible in 60 days.

The results were affirming. The Bible really is readable. More importantly, it's understandable.

One huge takeaway was the power of a particular teaching theme to help the Bible make sense – the Seed. This "Seed" theme has been shared all over the world to subscribers to my free online Bible reading journeys.

So I decided to create a reduced reading plan – 33% of the Bible – that keeps us focused on the Journey of the Seed.

That's what this book is about.

The purpose of this book

This book is a resource for your faith. Its goal is to help you do two things:

1. Read the Bible

2. Understand the Bible.

We're going to read the Bible together. Each day's reading takes 20-30 minutes per day. In 60 days you will have read one-third of the Bible!

Yes, that's cool.

You'll see just how readable the Bible really is. And when I say "read", I mean just read.

No homework. No scripture memory. No trick questions to test comprehension. Just read through the 60-day plan.

Each day I'll share a special insight from the reading segment that helps bring the Big Picture into view.

If you're a parent, this is a journey to involve your whole family.

And if you're a young person – young adult or teenager, or even younger – this is your chance to take ownership of your walk with God. You can read the Bible! And you can understand it too.

My daughter read this plan as a ten-year old. Of course she didn't understand everything – I don't either. But it's amazing just how much we can understand, even at a young age.

While I'm honored to help facilitate this experience, it's really our special teacher that does all the work.

And now finally, let me introduce you to our new Teacher!

Meet our teacher, The Seed

When I shared the "special talk" (yes, s-e-x) with my sons years ago, I didn't use "birds and bees." I talked specifically about the "seed" - the Seed from a daddy and a mommy that results in a baby.

I've found the "seed" to be a helpful tool when I want to transition to talking about the Bible.

The Bible is about The Seed.

A launch pad for this Seed theme is Genesis 3:15: The Seed of the woman will one day defeat the enemy and save the world.

And I will put enmity
Between you and the woman,
*And between your **seed** and her **seed**;*
He shall bruise you on the head,
And you shall bruise him on the heel." (NASB)

God is talking to the serpent – that's Satan, the devil. The woman is Eve, "mother of all the living." And the "seed" of the woman is her offspring, a human child.

This human child grows up and has their own offspring, who grows up and has their own offspring... and so on. From the "seed" of the woman comes a very special Seed - Jesus Christ.

After Adam and Eve are tempted in the garden by the serpent, sin enters the world. God tells the serpent,

"Satan, your fate is sealed! For a season, you will be allowed to harass my creation. You will be a nuisance to the world. Like a pesky mosquito, you will strike the heel of The Seed. But one day, this Seed will crush your head. And you will be done... forever." [Jeff paraphrase of Genesis 3:15]

Journey of The Seed

For 60 days we're going to follow The Seed's journey. The journey of The Seed presents an epic battle between good and evil. It's a grander story than could be scripted by any Hollywood movie.

The Seed helps to understand the flow of the Bible. God's story follows the history of The Seed family.

The Seed helps to understand the interconnectedness of the main characters. If the Bible is a play script, The Seed Family is the cast.

The Seed helps to explain some of our big questions (i.e. why was there so much killing and warfare in the Old Testament?) The Seed also helps to appreciate some of the seemingly dry genealogies and geographies. The Seed is an amazing teacher of the Bible. With the help of The Seed, we'll piece together a Big-picture narrative of the Bible.

Over the past few years I have been helping people to read and understand the Bible. But it really isn't Jeff doing the teaching. It's The Seed.

The Seed has been teaching children, parents and grandparents. The Seed teaches seekers of the faith and life-long Bible readers.

The Seed is a simple theme. Readers of all ages and faith levels are experiencing breakthroughs in faith by finally being able to read the Bible – but more importantly, by understanding its central theme.

When you embrace this 60-day journey, I trust you'll never see the Bible the same way again. And most importantly, you'll want to read through the Bible again…and again.

Let's begin.

The Seed Defined

Here's a guide for various references to the "Seed" throughout this book.

- ➤ seed – generic reference to offspring. (i.e. Abraham's seed, David's seed, seed of the woman, etc.)

- ➤ The Seed – refers to the line of offspring from Adam to Christ; there are over 60 fathers in the line of "The Seed"; these descendants come from the line of Judah (one of twelve tribes of Israel).

- ➤ The SEED – this all-cap expression refers to Jesus Christ, the 2nd Adam; final offspring in the line of "The Seed."

- ➤ Seed Family – used occasionally to reference the broader nation of Israelites. While "The Seed" is limited to 64 specific ancestors from the tribe of Judah, the broader Seed Family consists of the entire twelve tribe alliance. Together, these other tribes play a significant role in protecting The Seed.

The Bible's Big Picture

So what is the Bible's big picture? What's a simple narrative to help us track the Bible's central theme and key focal points?

The Bible is about the Journey of The Seed

- that travels through 4,000 years,

- consisting of roughly 60+ generations,

- connected by six (6) key reset events,

- focused on two (2) resurrection events,

- which set up one (1) final climactic redemptive event: the recreation of the Heavens and the Earth.

Let's break it down.

4,000 Years: God could have dealt with the serpent immediately. He could have ended this head-crushing episode much sooner. Jesus could have been born directly to Adam and Eve, or maybe a few generations later.

Instead, God waited roughly 4,000 years to deliver The SEED to earth in the form of a man, Jesus.

God gives us the data to calculate this 4,000-year Biblical timeline. Third graders can chart the date of Noah's flood with a calculator, some paper and the text from Genesis 5. (I'll show you how do to this later).

What's mostly viewed as a bland string of "begats" (so-and-so begat so-and-so who begat so-and-so...), is actually God's gift to help us construct a Bible timeline.

Throughout scriptures, God provides helpful references to piece together the Bible's timeline.

Over 60 Generations: I like to ask kids, "how many great, great, great…. grandfathers does it take to track the "Seed" from Christ to Adam?

They might say thousands, or tens of thousands… or even millions.

Actually the number of fathers in the line of the 1st Adam to the 2nd Adam (Jesus) is less than 100.

The Gospel of Luke traces the genealogy from Adam to Mary – 75 generations. Matthew's Gospel builds a partial genealogy from Abraham to Joseph. The Bible reveals 64 generations from Adam to Jesus.

Think of the Bible as a collection of birth certificates of each generation from Adam to Christ.

Take a look at The Seed Chart in the next section of the book. This chart will be a helpful reference throughout our 60-day journey.

6 "Reset" Events: It's easy to become numb to the Bible's miraculous stories. God saves a single family from a global flood, parts the waters to save the Israelites, helps a young shepherd boy to kill a giant with a small stone.

Bible stories are important. We should teach them to our children. The problem is, we often teach them with no context for how they relate to the big picture

These events are not just cool Bible stories for kids. Many of them serve as massive "resets", events that reset the direction and path for The Seed to travel.

While Satan is trying to kill The Seed, God is plotting its survival. When Satan makes an attack, God often responds with a miracle event to carry The Seed to safety.

Consider the escape from Egypt. The Seed Family (Israelites) was under the oppression of slavery. Even genocide attempts sought to wipe them out.

But God rescued the Israelites through a man named Moses. It's not just a neat story with ten plagues. It was a masterful escape plan, resetting a new path for The Seed to grow and prosper.

Be sure to flag the "Reset" chart in the next section. We'll encounter these resets events throughout our reading.

Two resurrection events: These events are integral to the overall biblical narrative.

The resurrection of Jesus Christ: The SEED (Jesus) came to earth to die a sacrificial death. It was God's plan from the beginning, a part of His "head-crushing" strategy to defeat the serpent. Three days after his cross crucifixion, Jesus was resurrected from the dead. A stunning miracle! This makes possible the next resurrection event.

The resurrection of the Dead: One day in the future, Jesus will return in the sky to "rapture" the saints into heaven. Those who have entrusted their faith and life in The SEED will have their names written in the Lamb's Book of Life and one day experience their own bodily resurrection.

One final climactic event: This event lies ahead of us as well – the recreation of the heavens and the earth. The event follows the final judgment and destruction of Satan, his angels, and all those whose names are not written in the Book of Life.

One more time

The Bible is about the Journey of The Seed

that travels through 4,000 years,

consisting of roughly 60+ generations,

organized around six (6) key reset events,

focused on two (2) resurrection events,

*that set up one (1) final, climactic redemptive event...the recre-
ation of the Heavens and the Earth.*

Receiving the Best Results

1. Read quickly – This is not Bible study or scripture meditation. This is Bible "reading." And I suggest you read quickly. I call it Power Reading.

Don't worry about what you don't understand. Lock in to a fast pace and you'll be surprised just how much you will understand.

And consider this - Bible reading is a life long activity. This won't be your last time to read so whatever is not clear to you this time through, you'll have opportunity to build on your understanding in future readings.

For more about the *Power Read* idea see my blogs and articles at www.PowerReadtheBible.com

2. Use the tools! The next chapter includes the 60-day reading plan as well as various charts and visual aids to help you along the journey. Refer to them as needed to keep the Big Picture in view.

3. Journey with a group – Assemble a group to read through the 60-day plan with you. Gather together weekly or bi-weekly and use the discussion questions at the end of various daily summaries to spark conversation with your group.

You can also obtain Facilitator Outlines for free at www.PowerReadTheBible.com/Resources/ .

4. Keep a Weekly Focus – The Reading Plan is organized around a weekly flow that charts the course of The Seed. Keep this flow in mind as you journey through the reading plan.

Week	Theme	Section of Bible
1	The Beginning, the Patriarchs	Law (Pentateuch)
2	Escape from Egypt, the Law	Law (Pentateuch)
3	The Promised Land and Judges	History
4	The Kings - race to the top	History
5	The Kings - race to the bottom	History
6	Release from Captivity; Prophets	History, Prophets
7	The Gospels	Gospels
8	NT History	History
9	Revelation	Apocalypse

60-Day Reading Plan and Tools

33% Reading Plan

Day	Date	Daily Reading
1		Genesis 1-7
2		Genesis 8-14
3		Genesis 15-21
4		Genesis 22-28
5		Genesis 29-35
6		Gensis 36-42
7		Genesis 43-50
8		Exodus 1-7
9		Exodus 8-15
10		Exodus 16-20; 32-34; Lev 26
11		Numbers 1, 3, 9-14
12		Numbers 15-18, 21, 26, 27
13		Deuteronomy 1-7
14		Deut. 8-11, 28, 30, 31, 34
15		Joshua 1-8
16		Joshua 9-14; 23-24
17		Judges 1-8
18		Judges 9-16
19		Judges 17-21; Ruth 1-4
20		1 Samuel 1-7
21		**Off/Catch-up Day**
22		1 Samuel 8-15
23		1 Samuel 16-23
24		1 Samuel 24-31
25		2 Samuel 1-8
26		2 Samuel 9-16
27		2 Samuel 17-24
28		1 Kings 1-5, 8-10

29		1 Kings 11
30		**Off/Catch-up Day**
31		1 Kings 12-18
32		1 Kings 19 - 2 Kings 3
33		2 Kings 4-11
34		2 Kings 12-17
35		2 Kings 18-25
36		Ezra 1-8
37		Ezra 9-10; Nehemiah 1-6
38		Nehemiah 7-13
39		Isaiah 1-9
40		Jeremiah 18-25
41		Jeremiah 26-34
42		Daniel 1-6
43		**Off/Catch-up Day**
44		Matthew 1-4
45		Luke 1-3
46		John 1-7
47		John 8-14
48		John 15-21
49		**Off/Catch-up Day**
50		Acts 1-7
51		Acts 8-14
52		Acts 15-21
53		Acts 22-28
54		Hebrews 1-7
55		Hebrews 8-13
56		**Off/Catch-up Day**
57		Revelation 1-6
58		Revelation 7-12
59		Revelation 13-18
60		Revelation 19-22

THE BIBLE'S BIG PICTURE TIMELINE

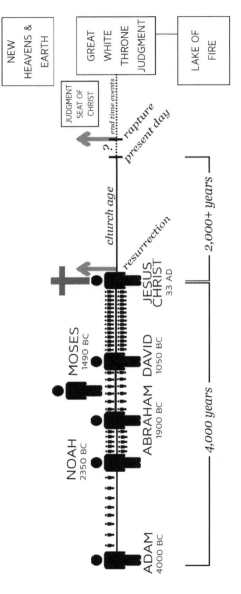

NEW HEAVENS & EARTH

GREAT WHITE THRONE JUDGMENT

LAKE OF FIRE

JUDGMENT SEAT OF CHRIST

end time events

rapture

present day

church age

resurrection

JESUS CHRIST
33 AD

MOSES
1490 BC

ABRAHAM
1900 BC

DAVID
1050 BC

NOAH
2350 BC

ADAM
4000 BC

4,000 years

2,000+ years

THE BIBLE IS ABOUT

*the journey of **THE SEED** that travels through **4,000** years, consisting of **65** generations, connected by **6** key 'resets', focused on **2** resurrection events, which set up **1** final, climactic, redemptive event...*

THE RECREATION OF THE HEAVENS AND EARTH

TRACKING "THE SEED"

1. Adam
2. Seth
3. Enos
4. Cainan
5. Mahalaleel
6. Jared
7. Enoch
8. Methuselah
9. Lamech
10. Noah
11. Shem
12. Arphaxad
*   Cainan
13. Salah
14. Eber
15. Peleg
16. Reu
17. Serug
18. Nahor
19. Terah
20. Abraham
21. Isaac

22. Jacob
23. Judah
24. Perez
25. Hezron
26. Ram
27. Amminadab
28. Nahshon
29. Salmon
30. Boaz
31. Obed
32. Jesse
33. David
34. Solomon
35. Rehoboam
36. Abijah
37. Asa
38. Jehoshaphat
39. Joram
40. Ahaziah
41. Joash
42. Amaziah
43. Azzariah (Uzziah)

44. Jotham
45. Ahaz
46. Hezekiah
47. Manasseh
48. Amon
49. Josiah
50. Jehoiakim
51. Jechoniah
52. Salathiel
53. Zerubbabel
54. Abiud
55. Eliakim
56. Azor
57. Sadoc
58. Achim
59. Eliud
60. Eleazar
61. Matthan
62. Jacob
63. Joseph
64. Jesus

* Name not reflected in Genesis or Chronicles genealogies, but recorded by Luke

[Footnote: Genealogy from "A Family Tree: from Adam to Jesus" copyright © 2014, Genesis Japan https://usstore.creation.com/genealogy-poster]

Key Biblical Resets

Who	What	(1) Threat	(2) Solution	(3) Key Sacrifice	(4) God's Promise
Adam [Reset 1]	The Fall	Sin/Death (Gen 2:17, 3:19, 22-24)	New Plan (3:15)	(Gen 3:21 – God made skins)	"My Seed will crush you, Satan" (Gen 3:15)
Noah [Reset 2]	The Flood	Wickedness (Gen 6:1-5)	Destroy earth/life – New Family to keep Seed Alive (Gen 6:6-13)	Noah's burnt offering (Gen 8:20)	Never again will I destroy the earth (Gen 8:21)
Abraham [Reset 3]	Father of Nations	More wickedness (general – i.e. Gen 13:13)	New Nation –pathway for The Seed	Various (Sacrifice of Isaac most familiar)	Land, offspring, blessings
				a. Gen 12:7 – built an altar	a. Gen 12:1-3
				b. Gen 13:18	b. Gen 13:14-17
				c. Gen 15:7-11	c. Gen 15:1-21
				d. Gen 17:9-14*	d. Gen 17:1-14
				e. Sacrifice of Isaac (Gen 22:15-18)	e. Gen 22:1-14
Moses [Reset 4]	Freedom from Egyptians	Slavery (Ex 1:6-14)	New Freedom - Escape from Egyptians (Ex 3:1-12)	Passover lamb/10th plague (Ex 12:1-13, 21-27)	If you will walk in my ways, all will go well (Lev 26, Deut 28)
David [Reset 5]	Forever Kingdom	N/A	N/A New Kingdom (chosen line of Kings)	Offerings for the Temple (1 Chron. 29)	I will establish your throne forever – (1 Chron. 17:11-12, 1 Chron 28:6-8; 2 Chron 6:16, 2 Sam 7:12-17, 1 Kings 2)
Jesus Christ [Reset 6]		King Herod (Matt 2:1-11)	Escape to Egypt (Matt 2:12-15, 19-23)		A child will be born, he will reign forever, his kingdom will have no end (Luke 1:30-33, 35, Matt 1:21/22, John 3, Jer 23:5, 33:15)
	(It is) Finished			Cross crucifixion (1 Cor 5:7, 1 Pet 1:19, Heb 9:11-14, 10:5-7)	Whoever believes in him shall not perish, but have eternal life (J316)

*circumcision instituted

DAILY SUMMARIES

DAY 0

THE SEED

[Read the day before beginning the 60-day plan.]

Greetings! Tomorrow begins our 60-day journey. To kick things off, I have a question to consider.

What's the most popular verse in the Bible?

When I ask a room of children this question, everyone blurts out "John 3:16!" According to Google, they may be right.

Then I ask, "What's the most popular verse in the Old Testament?" I may hear Jeremiah 29:11… or Joshua 1:9…or Proverbs 3:5. Good guesses.

While not the most popular, perhaps the most <u>foundational</u> verse in the Old Testament is Genesis 3:15.

And I will put enmity between you and the woman, and between your offspring and hers; he will crush your head, and you will strike his heel. (NIV)

When God cursed the serpent after Adam and Eve had sinned, He delivered a verdict and a forecast of what was to come.

There's going to be a **SEED**—Jesus—who will come from the line of Eve. The serpent (Satan) will harass the earth and strike the heel of Jesus. In the end, Jesus will crush Satan's head.

Genesis 3:15 is arguably the most common stop-by verse for Bible theologians used to explain the Bible's systematic theology.

From Genesis 3:15 forward, the rest of the Bible is all about working out this verse.

And sure enough, sixty-plus generations after Adam, this Holy Spirit **"SEED"** is born – baby Jesus. Jesus grows up, walks the earth, dies a crucifixion death and miraculously rises again.

This resurrection event is a crushing blow to the serpent, but not the final blow. (Spoiler alert!) That comes in the book of Revelation.

Genesis 3:15 is a mind-numbing prophecy and sums up the Bible narrative in less than 30 words.

As you read tomorrow, and throughout these next 60 days, keep the big picture in mind.

DAY 1

WHY DID GOD FLOOD THE EARTH?

[Scheduled Reading: Genesis 1-7]

After the creation account (Genesis 1 & 2), the fall (chapter 3), and account of the first ten generations (chapters 4 & 5) – we arrive at a shocking story (chapters 6 & 7).

God wipes out life on earth with a global flood. Why?! Geeez, this seems so extreme.

Scriptures actually say, "God was sorry that he had made man on the earth, and it grieved him to his heart" (Gen 6:6-7).

God actually regretted his creation. Stunning words!

Something was seriously wrong with this generation. They weren't just being naughty children – fighting with their siblings and talking mean to one another.

God has endured plenty of wickedness over the past 6,000 years but something with this pre-flood generation reached a boiling point and God said, "That's Enough!"

Genesis 6:1-4 gives us a clue: Sons of God marrying and pro-creating with daughters of man. What does this mean?

There are a few theories, but most involve some forms of angelic or demonic interference with the human race (seed).

To us, this feels like a sci-fi movie – and hardly believable. (Feel free to do your own research).

But if we take a moment to consider the idea, we can see how this would have been a brilliant strategy by the serpent.

Satan is shrewd and understands the Genesis 3:15 curse. He will do anything to corrupt the integrity of The Seed.

Remember, The SEED is a human descendant (this is Jesus) from Adam and Eve who will one day appear to save mankind from the curse of sin.

Angels intermarrying with the human race is a shrewd strategy to attack The Seed and take rebellion against God to a whole new level.

Here's the big idea for us to remember – throughout the rest of the Bible, there's a continual state of warfare being waged against God and His Seed strategy.

Throughout the next sixty days, we'll continue to look at this enmity, or hostility, from this Seed perspective.

Paper and Pencil Exercise

The Flood of Noah is perhaps the most dramatic of God's Seed-setting events in history.

Using the charts on page 27 and the text from Genesis 5 & 11, calculate the years from Adam to the flood. Do the same to calculate the timeline from Noah to Abraham.

Does it make sense that God would give us this data to help us calculate a biblical timeline?

DAY 2

ZERO TO SIXTY!

[Scheduled Reading: Genesis 8-14]

Today we reach #20. What's #20 you ask? That's Abraham - the 20th person in the line of The Seed.

We're tracking The Seed from Adam to Christ, just over sixty generations.

From Adam to Noah are 10 generations. Then from Shem (Noah's son) to Abraham are 10 more generations.

Genesis 5 and 11 gives us a nice genealogy for tracking The Seed. So already, two days into our read, we cover one-third of the 60+ names of The Seed!

These 20 generations span the period of two thousand years. But when we get to Abraham – the biblical story slows down.

The life of Abraham serves as a crucial pivot point for the path of The Seed. God has in mind, a special person and a special place.

-   The Person - God promised to route The Seed through Abraham. In a very forward-looking manner, God picks out a man to become father to many nations – most specifically the nation of Israelites.

-   The Place - God shifts the geography for The Seed. Relocating Abram's family from Ur (near Babylon) to Canaan was a huge pivot point. Jesus would eventually be born in the land of Canaan. Up until the life of Abraham, The Seed had been in the Mesopotamian region of Babylon.

Let's talk about it

How does the idea of "Tracking The Seed" impact your perspective of the Bible's Big Picture?

DAY 3

GOOD GUYS AND BAD GUYS

[Scheduled Reading: Genesis 15-21]

The biblical story is like a western movie. There are good guys and bad guys. In the current scene, Abraham and Lot are good guys. And there are lots of bad-guy characters – like the men of Sodom and Gomorrah.

In God's eyes, they're bad guys because they stand in direct opposition to God – and in opposition to advancing The Seed.

God sends two angels to destroy the two cities. When the angels visit Lot to rescue him, every man of the city surrounds Lot's house and threatens to break in and rape the angels.

If this still feels like a violent movie, I agree.

Then we come across one of the most unfathomable verses in the Bible.

Lot offers to give his virgin daughters to the bad guys as a compromise to leave the angels alone.

Now there isn't any explanation that can help me fully understand this sort of compromise. But here's a partial explanation as to what Lot might have been thinking.

Remember on Day 1 when we discussed the evil being carried out in the day of Noah? Sons of God were intermarrying daughters of men.

Could it be that Lot was well aware of the stories from the flood and the reason why God's wrath unleashed a flood of destruction?

Perhaps Lot saw that an angry mob wanting to sexually violate his angel visitors was a recipe for disaster.

The last time angels and humans interacted in such ways, God destroyed the earth with a flood.

In this case, the sons of man wanted to rape the sons of God, the angels. This sexual violation against God's angels was terrorizing to Lot.

I still can't understand how he would offer up his virgin daughters. (*Couldn't the angels take care of themselves anyway?*)

But here's the overall point for today. **The account of Sodom and Gomorrah is the second act of mass destruction in Bible history (the first being Noah's flood).**

In both instances, sexual immorality was the context.

God was serious about protecting The Seed. And protecting The Seed meant protecting His design for sex and procreation.

God was also strategic about geography. He relocated Abram's family from Ur to inhabit the land of Canaan. Eventually Christ would be born and raised in Canaan.

When God rained burning sulfur and fire from heaven to wipe out an entire community, He was cleaning out the land for the eventual arrival of the Israelites.

Sodom and Gomorrah were located in the land of Canaan (The Promised Land, the future of Israel). Their evil and wickedness was a threat to the path and future survival of The Seed.

As we read throughout the Old Testament and encounter more of God's destruction, keep this in mind – the role of God's wrath was not only to inflict punishment, but to clean out the land and make way for The Seed.

DAY 4

FORESHADOW

[Scheduled Reading: Genesis 22-28]

God charts the path of The Seed through Abraham – and keeps it on His chosen course.

Abraham has two sons (Ishmael and Isaac), but God chooses the line of **Isaac #21**. Isaac has two sons (Esau and Jacob), but God chooses the line of **Jacob #22**.

Let's look at the legacy of Isaac.

The parallels between Isaac and Jesus are stunning. Both arrive by divine birth.

Isaac was born to Abraham and Sarah in their very old age. Jesus was born to Mary, an unwed mother impregnated by a seed from heaven (conceived by the Holy Spirit).

Another parallel is a famous self-sacrifice. (Genesis 22) When God asked Abraham to sacrifice his son Isaac, it was an unthinkable request. Would God really require such a thing?

Abraham was committed to obedience. Isaac (somewhere between being an adolescent boy and a young man) was old enough to be a willing participant as he carried the wood on his shoulders to the place of worship.

This story is one we struggle to fully appreciate. It's far outside the realm of anything that's ever been requested by God. In fact, it just might be the most ridiculous request ever.

Scriptures are full of seemingly bizarre instructions from God. But nothing fits the category of "sacrifice your only son."

Especially if the son was a miracle child born to parents of old age – and the son through whom God promised to birth a nation!

But Abraham and Isaac cooperated. God stopped Abraham short of sacrificing Isaac and provided a ram for the blood sacrifice instead.

So what did God have in mind for this sacrifice request?

It was a scene that would unfold 2,000 years later. Jesus would carry his wood (a cross) up a nearby hill for his own sacrifice. Unlike with Abraham and Isaac, God did go through with the crucifixion death of His Son.

The near sacrifice of Isaac was a foreshadowing – a picture - of a future sacrifice (Jesus on the cross).

Isaac demonstrated obedience and submission to the same act that would one day become the most selfless act known to man.

How impressive was Isaac's almost-sacrifice? You could even say Jesus had an advantage that Isaac did not.

Jesus knew the outcome and purpose of his death on the cross. Isaac was not so sure. He was clueless. He was simply trusting God…with his life.

How fitting that God would route the path of The Seed through a man (Abraham) and his son (Isaac) – two men who would demonstrate unusual faith to carry out a similar sacrifice that God and Jesus would one day perform.

Stunning story. Stunning symbolism. Stunning faith.

DAY 5

12 SONS, 12 TRIBES

[Scheduled Reading: Genesis 29-35]

Jacob lived a high-drama life. He grew up competing with his twin brother, Esau (eventually stealing his birthright).

He worked seven years for a wife he didn't choose – then another seven years for the wife he did choose.

He wrestled with an angel of God.

He received a famous name change (from Jacob to "Israel").

His sons wreaked havoc on his family. They kidnapped their younger brother (the favored son, Joseph), sold him off to slavery and fabricated a story about a deadly animal attack.

(Does this count as a dysfunctional family?)

Still, Jacob's most significant life contribution might just be his twelve problematic sons. These twelve sons (born of two wives and two maidservants) resulted in twelve mighty tribes.

As we'll see in upcoming reading sessions, these tribes would become God's strategy for organizing and protecting the new nation of "Israel," (the Israelites).

And protecting Israel meant protecting The Seed!

Back to the big picture. While Satan was working feverishly to destroy The Seed, God was building them for survival.

Like any thriving nation, this Israelite nation would one day need to be strong, independent, well financed, heavily armed. They would need government that could sustain order.

God will accomplish these functions through the twelve-tribe alliance. In future chapters, we'll see the member tribes work together to share land, share a unified army, share governance, share in the welfare of the poor and widows, etc.

Much like the thirteen colonies that would one day govern the new America, these twelve tribes will govern a new nation called Israel.

Back to our reading. It sure doesn't seem like anything special can come from Jacob's clan. They were a very dysfunctional and chaotic bunch.

But as we'll see, God is about to launch an impressive historical movement from this family.

Who would you choose?

There are twelve tribes (sons) of Jacob.

But only one of the tribes can transfer The Seed.

Which tribe do you think will have that special honor?

Who would you choose?

Stay tuned.

DAY 6
BIZARRE INTERRUPTIONS

[Scheduled Reading: Genesis 36-42]

There are some strange stories in the Bible.

As you read certain accounts you might even wonder, "Why is this story here?"

Often, it's simply because of God's pattern of tracking The Seed —the family tree from Adam to Christ.

This happens just as we're getting settled into the life story of Joseph. Then a bizarre interruption appears for Bible readers. (Welcome to Genesis 38).

Jesus came from Abraham, Isaac, Jacob, Judah... then baby Perez, the child of Tamar.

And who exactly was this mother, Tamar? Well, it's quite a story!

Perez was conceived when his father, Judah, visited a pretending prostitute, who unbeknownst to him was his daughter-in-law, Tamar!

The short story is this: Judah's first two sons were killed by God because of their wickedness (not a very impressive parenting legacy).

According to tradition, Judah was expected to commit his third son to the widow of his deceased sons. (Tamar was the widow to the first son, and then the second son.)

In this way, the Israelites fulfilled the duty of keeping the family name alive.

But Judah and Son #3 (Shelah) did not cooperate. So in God's divine and seemingly odd ways, He arranged for Judah an encounter with a lady disguised as a prostitute – who turned out to be his daughter-in-law, Tamar!

I know. Surprise!

Through Judah, Tamar had twin boys. The oldest, and the one in the line of The Seed, was baby Perez.

Stories like these show God's amazing sovereignty... and His desire to reveal for us the genealogy of Jesus Christ.

DAY 7

GOD'S SOVEREIGNTY

[Scheduled Reading: Genesis 43-50]

One thing we learn about the path of The Seed: God does not always choose the logical path – at least not from our perspective.

If I were to choose the path of The Seed from the twelve sons of Jacob, I would choose Joseph - a man of impeccable character, with an impressive faith and work resumé.

He saved his family from a famine – even after they kidnapped and sold him years earlier.

But God didn't route The Seed through Joseph. God chose Judah, one of the older brothers (one of the kidnappers!)

Years after the kidnapping, Joseph rose to power in Egypt (fascinating story covering Genesis chapters 37, 39-47).

During a dreadful famine in Canaan, Jacob sent his dysfunctional sons to Egypt to buy food. Their shocking encounter with Joseph set up an eventual family reunion – the brothers returned home to get Jacob and went back to live with Joseph in Egypt.

This detour to Egypt is a monumental pivot for The Seed – a survival measure orchestrated by God to keep The Seed alive.

Just before Jacob died he delivered a blessing to each of his twelve sons.

Judah's blessing reveals God's chosen path for The Seed.

The scepter shall not depart from Judah, nor the ruler's staff from between his feet, until tribute comes to him (Genesis 49:10).

The tribe of Judah would be represented by a line of kings...an eventual king who's reign will never end – King Jesus!

Jesus came from the Tribe of Judah. Judah's legacy echoes into the future.

As we learned yesterday, Judah's actual life story was quite an embarrassment to the family tree. His legacy was not defined by honor or faith or leadership or military exploits.

Instead Judah was known for one of the Bible's classic family scandals.

But that doesn't matter. When it comes to the path of The Seed, God's sovereignty prevails. And God chooses the line of Judah.

Big Picture Recap

We just finished Genesis! The biblical story (and The Seed) started in the Garden of Eden. A few hundred years after the flood "reset", God led a man named Abram from Ur to Canaan.

Then after a famine, Abraham's grandson (Jacob) and great-grandsons flee to Egypt where Joseph rises to power. It's been roughly 2,000 years and The Seed is resting with a person named Hezron (#25 – See Genesis 46:12).

DAY 8

ANOTHER SEED ATTACK

[Scheduled Reading: Exodus 1-7]

As we enter a new book (Exodus), immediately there's another assault on The Seed.

The Pharaoh of Egypt is killing baby boy Israelites. Let's put this in seed language – the serpent is attempting to destroy members of The Seed Family.

Here's the context. After the family of Jacob (again, that's Israel) escaped the famine to Egypt to live with Joseph, the Israelite tribes grew… and grew and grew and grew.

Roughly two hundred years after the move to Egypt, all was forgotten of Joseph and his leadership in Egypt. The Israelites became despised by the Egyptians who feared the Israelites for their rapid growth.

First the Egyptians subjected the Israelites to harsh slavery. When that didn't curb the Israelite growth rate, the Pharaoh sent out his decree to exterminate the baby boys.

As we're learning in our Bible read – when bad guys start messing with God's Seed strategy, bad things start to happen.

God had in mind a series of nasty plagues to harass Pharaoh and the Egyptians. And God chose a man named Moses to interact with the Pharaoh.

This man Moses has one of the most decorated life stories of all the characters in the Bible.

As a newborn baby, Moses was placed in a basket and sent floating along the Nile River to escape the fate of the Pharaoh's death decree. His rescue by a princess sets up a stunning turn of events.

Baby Moses is actually nursed by his own mother and later grows up in the Pharaoh's palace.

Up until Abraham, the Bible has been mostly focused on characters in line of The Seed. From Adam to Noah to Abraham.... Isaac...Jacob... Judah.

Joseph was the first major Bible character who fell outside the direct path of The Seed.

Moses is the next significant Bible character who falls outside the line of The Seed.

Moses is not from the line of Judah but from the line of Levi (another of the 12 tribes).

This will make more sense later.

DAY 9

THE PASSOVER LAMB

[Scheduled Reading: Exodus 8-15]

Remember the "almost sacrifice" of Isaac – when God asked Abraham to sacrifice his son?

It was an incredible foreshadowing of a future event – when God would sacrifice His own son Jesus (The Seed) on a cross.

Today we encounter another of scriptures key foreshadowing events. It's the final of the ten plagues – the Passover sacrifice.

God delivers nine plagues, or attacks, on Pharaoh and the Egyptians. God has full control over Pharaoh's psyche and gets inside the man's head…and hardens his heart.

Finally, on "Passover night" the death angel passes through town to make a blood inspection at the entrance of all the homes. The sign of blood on the door was the signal that a male lamb had been sacrificed to the Lord for that household.

Later during the night the Egyptians awake to discover the death of the firstborn male in each household – because they had not known of the Passover instructions. (The Passover event was a special custom for just the Israelites.)

This was the final straw. Pharaoh had had enough with the Israelites and tells Moses to leave.

To encourage their departure, the Egyptians flood the Israelites with possessions on their way out of the country.

Then Pharaoh, God's string-puppet, changes his mind and chases the Israelites across the Red Sea passing.

Then God closes the waters and drowns out the Egyptians.

The story is dramatic and we enjoy teaching the history to our children.

But beneath the story is another stunning foreshadowing moment.

One day in the future, on the fourteenth day of the first month of the year (the Passover holiday) – a special lamb would be sacrificed.

Sure enough, roughly 1,500 years later – Jesus (The SEED) offered himself up as the Passover Lamb, the Lamb of God, for the sins of the world.

For Bible readers, the crucifixion event does not appear until the New Testament. But Old Testament readers get some sneak peak moments along the way.

The tenth plague (the killing of the firstborns on the first Passover) is one of those look-ahead moments.

Family Talk

Discuss how the Escape from Egypt served as a key "reset" for The Seed. Refer to chart on page 28.

DAY 10

CONGRATULATIONS!

[Scheduled Reading: Exodus 16-20, 32-34; Leviticus 26]

Today, I just want to say... Congratulations!

You're at Day 10 (smiles).

With some skipping around, we're going to get through Exodus and Leviticus today.

We're mostly fast-forwarding through some instructions for the Israelite community.

(These include laws & regulations, tabernacle instructions, special roles and duties of Levites, etc.)

Pay close attention to Leviticus 26. It lays out a fundamental promise that remains in play throughout the rest of the Old Testament.

It's a very straightforward promise. If the Israelites obey – good things will happen. If they disobey God – look out!

We'll circle back to this working premise throughout our read. It's crucial to understanding why God does what He does with the Israelites and The Seed journey.

DAY 11

ROLL CALL

[Scheduled Reading: Numbers 1, 3, 9-14]

The book of Numbers begins with a roll call... a census.

One year after the jailbreak from Egypt, God orders Moses to count all the men 20 years old or older. The census count numbers over 600,000 men.

Each of the tribes is counted, except for the tribe of Levi. The Levites are set apart to serve the system of worship and sacrifices for the Israelites.

For Bible readers, this is a monumental distinction to note.
God is a very sentimental God and enjoys deep symbolisms.
In God's mind, the Levites represent the "firstborn" of Israel – set apart for the purposes of God.

Symbolically, the Levites were to bear the sins of the people. By undergoing ceremonial cleanings, they would be authorized to receive the offerings of the remaining tribes.

It makes sense now why God chose a leader (Moses) from the tribe of Levi instead of the tribe of Judah. While the tribe of Judah carries The Seed into the future, the Levites had the responsibility to mange the administration and governance for the entire nation of Israel.

In Chapter 9 we have the second Passover Celebration (the first one was on the eve of the Exodus from Egypt).

From there, morale begins to slide. Complaining and disgruntledness becomes the new operating standard for the Israelites. And Moses becomes the whipping boy... the target of their rebuke.

God takes this personally – an attack against Moses is an attack against God.

God kills thousands of Israelites for their uprisings!

Ultimately God delivers a devastating indictment against the Israelites (Numbers 13 & 14).

A group of weak-willed spies returns from a 40-day visit to the Promised Land and spreads negative reports about the visit.

God's punishment is a 40-year time out. Instead of entering into Canaan (the Promised Land), they must wait 40 years for the adult generation to die off!

Only Joshua and Caleb, with the younger generation of Israelites, would be allowed to cross over.

Twelve Minus One – Is still Twelve

Periodically we'll encounter a listing of the tribes of Israel. For example, when the Promised Land is distributed, each tribe receives a land inheritance... except the Levites. That's because the Levites were set apart by God and were to receive the tithes and support from the other tribes.

But there are still 12 tribes that receive land. How is that so? Well, the tribe of Joseph is split between his two sons – the two half tribes of Manasseh and Ephraim.

DAY 12

TIME OUT

[Scheduled Reading: Numbers 15-18, 20, 21, 26, 27]

The Israelites are in a classic kindergarten time-out. They're not going anywhere for 40 years, except to wander around the wilderness, setting up and taking down the tent tabernacle whenever and wherever God moves the cloud.

They mope around with their heads hanging low, dragging their feet like rebellious teenagers.

After another rebellion episode (Chapter 16), God wants to kill everyone! (Stunning, isn't it!)

Moses pleads for God's mercy on behalf of the people – so God only kills roughly 15,000 people! (v16:49).

Moses also finds himself in hot water with God . After an unfortunate rock-striking incident (Chapter 20), Moses faces the same fate as the rest of the Israelite nation: he too will not be permitted to enter the Promised Land.

Near the end of the 40-year time out, God orders another census of the Israelite nation and instructs Moses to anoint Joshua as his successor.

So where exactly is The Seed during this 40-year season? Let's step back and take a look.

Hezron (#25), son of Perez was among the seventy people of the "house of Jacob" (Gen. 46:12, 26, 27) who traveled to Egypt to live with Joseph.

During this 215 year period in Egypt, **Ram (#26), Amminadab (#27)** and **Nahshon (#28)** were born (Ruth 4:18-20).

Nahshon was the assigned military commander of the tribe of Judah, assembled under the leadership of Moses (Num. 1:7, 2:3, 10:14).

Nahshon had command of a force of 74,600 men. That's impressive authority! (Num. 1:26, 2:4).

Nahshon was among the generation kept out of the Promised Land.

But Nahshon's son, Salmon, was likely among the "little ones" (Num. 14:31) who grew up and crossed into the Promised Land with Joshua and Caleb.

And what's so famous about Salmon (besides his fishy name)? We'll save that for later.

DAY 13

REVIEW SESSION

[Scheduled Reading: Deuteronomy 1-7]

In college I always appreciated review sessions – the chance to review what we had just studied or learned together. For us Bible readers, Deuteronomy is a review – a recap of all that had happened since they escape from Egypt.

Before Moses passes the baton to Joshua, Moses delivers the entire law again, this time to the 2nd generation of Israelites.

Exodus-Leviticus-Numbers contain the books of the law that cover the forty year period of wandering in the wilderness. Deuteronomy is a repeat of laws and history for the benefit of the new generation of Israelites.

Our reading plan omits some content in Exodus, Leviticus, Numbers & Deuteronomy. So what's been going on in these books?

Besides a 40-year time out, God is working a plan to route The Seed through the nation of Israel. From the time of Moses, it will be roughly 1,500 years until this eventual SEED (Jesus) takes its place on the cross.

While Satan is working feverishly to destroy the "seed" carriers (Israelites), God is building them for survival.

As mentioned earlier, this Israelite nation must be strong, independent, well financed, heavily armed. And they need a government that can sustain order. (Think about the U.S. We need those things, too.)

To set up this sustaining government, God gives them:

- **Label** – God calls them Israelites. He also calls Israel His "firstborn son." Extremely symbolic isn't it?

- **Land** - That's Canaan - the Promised Land! They wander in the wilderness for forty years before gaining entrance. Then the twelve tribes are counted in a census, and given their respective land allotments (we read this in Numbers).

- **Location (of worship)** - While wandering in the wilderness, whenever they stop to set up camp the tabernacle goes up. Detailed Bible text is committed to this elaborate tent design and related worship practices.

- **Laws** - God installs a system of sacrifices and laws to remind them of God's holiness, of their sin and of the way things ought to be had man never sinned. So if a young man skins his knee on a rock and suffers an open cut wound while playing with his kids, he is considered "unclean."

God wanted them to understand, "it wasn't intended to be this way" (skinning knees, that is). These laws were very detailed and often confusing…and sometimes weird.

- **Leader** - Yeah, that would be Moses. And eventually Joshua.

- **Levites** - This tribe is set apart to run the government, sort of like the U.S. congress. They manage the tabernacle, administer laws, perform sacrifices, etc. Their work is funded by a system of gifts and offerings from the other tribes.

Throughout the Old Testament, we'll see this system at work. It functions on occasion, but breaks down most of the time.

Still God's primary purpose is intact: keeping the nation of Israel alive… which means keeping The Seed alive.

Day 14
LEADERSHIP TRANSFER

[Scheduled Reading: Deuteronomy 8-11, 28, 30, 31, 34]

The most effective leadership transfer in the Old Testament might be the one between Moses and Joshua.

I heard a Bible teacher once refer to Joshua as "Mini Mo" (i.e. little Moses). Joshua was successor to Moses and took the Israelites into the Promised Land.

Both Moses and Joshua understood the importance of God's Word.

Throughout Deuteronomy, Moses strongly admonishes the Israelites to teach God's words to their children.

It's almost as if he knew they wouldn't (he knew them well) and that particular disasters would follow if they took their eyes off God.

Pay particular attention to Moses' charge to parents in Deuteronomy, Chapters 4, 6 and 11. (Here's the one in chapter 6.)

"Hear, O Israel: The Lord our God, the Lord is one. You shall love the Lord your God with all your heart and with all your soul and with all your might. And these words that I command you today shall be on your heart.

You shall teach them diligently to your children, and shall talk of them when you sit in your house, and when you walk by the way, and when you lie down, and when you rise." —Deuteronomy 6:4-7

In Deuteronomy 31, Moses commissions Joshua and instructs the Israelites to read the entire law publicly at the end of every seven years (verse 10-13).

Sure enough, some time later Joshua read the entire law to a public assembly, including *the women, and the little ones, and the sojourners* (Joshua 8:35).

Joshua was very mindful to help the Israelites pass the knowledge of God to the next generation (Joshua 4:6, 21).

I'm inspired to be like Moses and Joshua: to treasure God's Word, read it publicly in my home, and pass down the knowledge of God to the next generation in my family.

Blessings and Curses

Remember the condition of blessings and curses in Leviticus 26? If you obey – good fortune; If you disobey – disaster.

This theme is repeated in Deuteronomy 28.

And the theme is played out all through the Old Testament.

Mankind continues to fall back in touch with their rebellious nature. No matter how miraculous God's rescue and deliverance is, and how genuine the people's response of repentance and forgiveness, God's children seem to drift again... and again.

Sadly, this will be the fate of the Israelite nation.

DAY 15

FLINT KNIVES

[Scheduled Reading: Joshua 1-8]

We spent Week #1 in Genesis, covering roughly 2,000 years of Biblical history.

In Week #2 we cleared the remaining four books of the law, covering just 40 years – a single generation!

For the Israelites, it's time to break out of this wilderness rut and start living. And break out they do!

Here's a quick run down of the first several chapters:

Chapter 1 - Joshua assumes firm command of the Israelites.

Chapter 2 – A private company of men go on an exploratory mission to Jericho. They make a strategic connection with Rahab, the prostitute.

Chapter 3 – The Israelite nation crosses the Jordan River.

Chapter 4 – A memorial service is held.

Chapter 5 – All the men are circumcised. (Remember, the previous generation had died. So roughly 600,000 men were circumcised with flint knives! (Think about that).

While healing from their circumcision, they celebrate the Passover on the 14th day of the first month of the year.
Chapter 6 – This is where it gets interesting.

It's time for the dirty work to begin. God has plans for the Israelites to start taking enemy territories by storm.

These take-over campaigns don't sound like a loving and neighborly way to make friends – but we'll come back to that point in a few days. God prescribes a strange formula for this particular take-over.

Seven priests will blow seven trumpets while the army marches around the walls of Jericho for six straight days. On the seventh day, they march around the city seven times (God likes the number seven). The walls come down, the people flee and the Israelites devote all the inhabitants and animals to destruction with the sword. It must have been a nasty site.

One family is spared, the family of Rahab who cooperated with the spies during their takeover mission (chapter 2).

Rahab was instrumental in allowing Joshua's spies to penetrate the walls of Jericho, setting up its eventual fall.

Something else is special about this lady, Rahab. She eventually marries **Salmon** the son of Nahshon. And what's so special about Salmon? He's in the line of The Seed - **#29**. That's right. Rabah the harlot is in the line of Jesus Christ!

Honorable Mention

Remember Judah's strange encounter with his daughter-in-law Tamar? The story is in the Bible to trace the path of The Seed.

As is the case with Rahab – Tamar has her own role in Seed history. She's also one of only two mothers mentioned in Matthew's genealogy (see Matthew 1:5). She's also given special mention for her faith in the book of Hebrews (11:31).

DAY 16

FICKLE FAITH CYCLE

[Scheduled Reading: Joshua 9-14, 22-24]

There's a familiar pattern for the Israelites and we need to get used to it. It lasts throughout the entire Old Testament. It looks like this.

- God protects, provides and prospers His children.

- His children become content, complacent, and then turn from God in their sin.

- God withdraws His favor, punishes His children.

- The children are humbled, then repentant, then back on good terms with God again.

And the fickle faith cycle continues. This is the cycle for the nation as a whole, and for individuals as well. At times, even one man's sins could doom the entire nation.

Consider Joshua 7 & 8.

- One man (Achan) sins, God becomes angry.

- God withdraws protection and Israel is humiliated in a small battle.

- Israel calls out to God, repents, and punishes the offender (they stone Achan's family!)

- God's protection returns. Israel kicks tail in the next battle.

That's pretty much the life cycle of the Israelites ever since they escaped slavery in Egypt.

God rescues them from slavery. They become content. Then they complain about not having better food to each. God strikes them with plagues. They repent. Then the cycle starts over again.

Under Joshua, things are mostly stable. Joshua was both a great military commander and spiritual leader. Like Moses, he closes out his leadership life admonishing the people to cling close to the words of God (Joshua 23 & 24).

His leadership chant is among the most inspiring rally calls in scriptures. *As for me and my house, we will serve the Lord (Joshua 24:15).* Joshua's impressive leadership legacy is summed up by this single verse.

Israel served the Lord all the days of Joshua, and all the days of the elders who outlived Joshua and had known all the work that the Lord did for Israel. (Joshua 24:31)

Wow! But then just a few pages away in your Bible, you'll find a very sad passage.

And there arose another generation after them who did not know the Lord or the word that he had done for Israel (Judges 2:10).

The fickle faith journey continues.

Family Talk

Remember our discussion of Leviticus 26 & Deuteronomy 28 regarding blessings and curses?

Read Judges 2:1-3 & 11-15 and discuss how God's pattern for dealing with the Israelites fits this theme.

DAY 17

WHY ALL THE BLOODSHED?

[Scheduled Reading: Judges 1-8]

Let's step back and look at the big picture.

The goal for the twelve tribes was to inhabit a new land, a spacious land, a land flowing of milk and honey. It's the land of Canaan. The Promised Land.

God had that land in mind when he led Terah and Abram out of Ur, over five hundred years earlier.

After Joshua died and while settling in the Promised Land, the Israelites continued to encounter various enemy groups.

So God assigned military leaders – known as "judges" - to rally the twelve tribes and fight off these enemies.

For this era of "judges," don't think of pot-bellied men wearing robes. Think of MMA (mixed martial arts) fighters with swords. Some of these judges were legendary warriors!

Often reading through the Old Testament feels like an endless list of casualty records— big battles, and non-stop bloodshed. (While reading you're noticing some of these stories "Rated R for Intense Violence.")

What's the reason for all this death? And the bigger question: Why was God involved in helping the Israelites to wipe out their enemies?

It's all about The Seed. And it goes back to Genesis 3:15

And I will put enmity between you and the woman, and between your seed and her seed; He shall bruise you on the head, and you shall bruise him on the heel. (NASB)
Remember, Genesis 3:15 is a declaration of war.

And for 4,000 years God is working to transfer The Seed through history. Preserving the path for The Seed involves survival—keeping the lineage of Israel alive. And this means destroying enemies that stand in the way.

It's hard for us to relate to such violence today. But it's a testament to how God has preserved The Seed over the course of history.

As The Seed gets closer to the New Testament, the killing campaigns end.

But until then, the battle wages on. The Seed's ultimate arrival is over 1,000 years away in a nearby town of Bethlehem.

Establishing a presence in this land is mission critical for The Seed.

Family Talk

How does the perspective of the protecting and preserving The Seed help to make sense of the Bible's violence?

What questions might you still have about how God chose to handle this conflict?

DAY 18

FORTY YEARS

[Scheduled Reading: Judges 9-16]

For a football coach, the objective of the game is to score touch-downs on a 100-yard field. But you don't have to score in a single play.

Ten yards at a time will work just fine. Then the referees "move the chains." Then ten more yards, then move the chains again.

Eventually the team will be in the end zone (Score!).

In God's view, forward progress for The Seed seems to be about 40 years at a time.

The Israelites wandered in the wilderness for **40 years** before entry into the Promised Land. Joshua ruled them for 45 years.

After Joshua died, the fickle faith journey repeats – Israel does evil in the sight of the Lord (Judges 3:7).

What do God's people do when they encounter disaster? They call out to God (3:9).

So God raises up a deliverer named Othniel, the first of the era of judges. Under Othniel, the land of Israel receives rest for **40 years** (3:11).

But evil returns, followed by more affliction – Israel calls out to God again.

God gives then the next judge, Ehud. This time the land receives rest for 80 years (3:30).

As fickle faith would have it, the people turn to evil again. Judgment follows and then so does repentance.

Under the next judge, Deborah, the land of Israel has rest for another **40 years!** (5:31).

The cycle repeats, this time under a famous judge named Gideon. Then another **40 years** of rest (8:28).

Sometimes the rest was 40 years. And sometimes the punishment was 40 years.

Just before the famous judge Samson, God put Israel into the hands of the Philistines for **40 years** (13:1).

Even within Israel's fickle faith cycle – Samson is having his own fickle faith journey.

- God gives him strength and Samson gives God glory.
- Then Samson becomes lazy, loses his strength, becomes captured.
- Now desperate, Samson turns back to God. God gives Samson a final victory moment just before his death.

Not every cycle is 40 years. Some are longer, some are shorter. But in the book of Judges, these 40-year clips are strikingly common.

Just over 1,100 years remain until The SEED (Jesus) appears from heaven.

But God is not in a hurry. 40 years at a time will get The Seed in the end zone just fine.

DAY 19

FAMOUS MOTHER

[Scheduled Reading: Judges 17-21; Ruth 1-4]

So where is The Seed in the midst of all these 40-year cycles?

The era of judges (from the death of Joshua to the anointing of King Saul) is about three hundred years.

In the front half of this 300-year stretch lived a man named **Boaz** (**#30** in The Seed journey).

And who was Boaz's father? Salmon (#29) – the husband to Rahab the harlot, who aided the Israelites in the Jericho takeover.

Meanwhile, a widow named Ruth moves back to Bethlehem with her mother-in-law Naomi. Previously Ruth had moved away from Jerusalem with her husband's family to escape a famine in the land.

After her husband's death, Ruth returns to Jerusalem and later meets and marries Boaz of the tribe of Judah.

There are a few special notes about Ruth's role in The Seed journey:

-First, she's originally a Moabite. In other words, she's a foreigner (not among the twelve tribes of Israel).

-Secondly, she has a famous mother-in-law. Her first mother-in-law was Naomi. But after marrying Boaz, she has another mother-in-law (likely deceased): Rahab. Wow!

Rahab and Ruth - that's two special mothers, both of non-Israelite descent, in the line of The Seed!

-Finally, there's something very special just around the corner for The Seed. Ruth is Grandmother to a man named **Jesse (#32)**, which makes her Great Grandmother to King **David (#33)**.

No kidding! Check it out.

Now these are the generations of Perez: Perez fathered Hezron, Hezron fathered Ram, Ram fathered Amminadab, Amminadab fathered Nahshon, Nahshon fathered Salmon, Salmon fathered Boaz, Boaz fathered Obed, Obed fathered Jesse, and Jesse fathered David. (Ruth 4:18-22)

Ruth's role in the Bible's genealogy is stunning!

Special Note

Today's read includes the account of an almost wipe-out of one of the 12 tribes – the tribe of Benjamin.

A Levite's concubine was murdered by some Benjamites in an all-night rape. It was a heinous crime. The Levite followed up with an equally shocking response. The result was a full roll-out of all of Israel against their brother-tribe, the Benjamites.

Day 20

FAITH TRANSFER IS HARD

[Scheduled Reading: 1 Samuel 1-7]

We're about to wrap up the era of judges. Eli and Samuel are the final two judges before God institutes a new era of leadership – kings!

Unlike the MMA fighter types, Eli and Samuel function more as priestly figures.

There's a disturbing observation of the lives of Eli and Samuel.

It has to do with this idea of faith-transfer: transferring faith to their children.

Eli did not have proper command of his sons. As priest, Eli was a public spiritual figure and his sons were a dishonorable reflection on the priesthood

God appeared to the little boy Samuel one night to pass along a message to Eli.

The message was essentially this – "Eli, judgment is coming upon your household on account of your sons."

Sure enough, judgment struck – Eli's sons were killed. When Eli heard this, he himself fell over and died.

You would think that Samuel would have been taking parenting notes.

Samuel knew how important it was to transfer faith to the next generation. He was God's chosen messenger to share this special truth with Eli. And Samuel had front row seat to witness the eventual demise of Eli's sons.

But stunningly, Samuel finds himself in a similar parenting predicament.

When Samuel was old, he made his sons judges. But the elders of Israel rejected them for Samuel's sons did not walk in the ways of God as Samuel had done. (1 Samuel 8:1-5).

Samuel was crushed. Like Eli, Samuel failed to transfer active faith to his sons.

Faith transfer is hard. It is not automatic. That's why Moses and Joshua were so adamant about teaching their children to know the word of God.

This sad testimony of failed faith transfer serves as a warning for us today also.

Sadly, the era of judges ended because Samuel's sons did not demonstrate the spiritual leadership desired by the people.

Instead they wanted to be ruled by kings like the surrounding nations.

God did not consider this a good idea – but as often is with God's ways, He gave the Israelites what they wanted anyway.

DAY 21

FREE DAY

[No scheduled reading]

Enjoy your free day today. Or use it as a catch-up day.

We're three weeks into our reading journey together. The Seed is at the halfway mark with Jesse (#32) and David (#33).

King Saul takes the throne at 1095 B.C. The Seed still has a ways to go and God is still taking His time.

We see some more 40-year ticks ahead:
- After Eli judges Israel for 40-years (1 Samuel 4:18) and then 12 years by Samuel,
- David rules Israel for 40 years(1 Kings 2:11).
- Then Solomon rules Israel for 40 years (1 Kings 11:42).

Again, this 40-year interval is not a rule. But this frequent period of time reminds us that God is moving The Seed from one generation to the next.

DAY 22

CONNECTING THE DOTS

[Scheduled Reading: 1 Samuel 8-15]

Am I not a Benjamite, from the least of the tribes of Israel? And is not my clan the humblest of all the clans of the tribe of Benjamin? (1 Samuel 9:21)

King Saul was from the tribe of Benjamin. They were supposedly the least of the tribes of Israel.

What made this tribe so weak?

Let's go back a few days to a story in Judges 20.

It involves a nasty fight that follows a most gruesome story about a Levite who cut up his dead concubine into twelve pieces and sent her throughout all the remaining tribes of Israel.

(The Levite's concubine had been murdered by some Benjaminites in an all-night rape.)

This was before Wiki-leaks and fake news, but I'm sure rumors were still strong.

When folks learned this event wasn't fake news, it got all of them fired up... against the Benjamites.

400,000 Israelites (from the remaining tribes) took on 26,000 Benjamites. It was a blood-bath. Over 25,000 Benjamite men were lost at battle, leaving 600 men running for the hills.

The tribe was nearly wiped out. It was a sad day for Israel.

Now we know what Saul means when he referred to himself as from the "least of the tribes of Israel." He meant it literally.

Not only in size, but the social stigma of being from the tribe of Benjamin was not exactly a badge of honor.

Throughout scriptures, we see that God will use anyone to accomplish his purposes.

He might choose a leader from the smallest tribe (like Saul). But he might choose a leader with striking appearance (again Saul).

Or he might choose a leader from the largest tribe (Judah) and one of lesser impressive appearances (that's David.)

God's selection process is God's business. Sometimes it makes sense to us. Other times it does not.

Sometimes he even regrets his choice (that's a strange idea, isn't it?)

And that's exactly what happens with the selection of Saul.

God is getting ready to abort his choice of King Saul and replace Him with a very special character.

Family Talk

God gave Israel a king even though it was not in their best interest (See Deut. 17:11-20).

What does this say about God's willingness to give us what we want, even if it's not God's best for us?

DAY 23

BIG

[Scheduled Reading: 1 Samuel 16-23]

Who would you consider among the list of the most famous ancestors to Jesus Christ?

Adam? Noah? Abraham, Isaac and Jacob?

Make room for King David. His role and legacy is gigantic!

Everything about David's life was BIG.

His dreams were BIG.

The giant he faced was BIG.

The battles he fought were BIG.

His fame was BIG. His enemies were BIG.

The sin he committed was BIG.

The fallout from his sin was BIG.

His vision to build God a house was BIG.

His family was BIG.

His bodyguards were BIG.

His sacrifices were BIG.

His praises were BIG (check out the book of Psalms)

When reading about King David, it's hard to not fall into a trance and feel like the stories we're reading are the make-believe kind. But they're not. They happened.

Something else was BIG. God's covenant with David.

We're not there yet, but we will be soon.

This upcoming covenant with David is among the most significant Seed-directing events in the Bible – right up there with Noah's flood and the Abrahamic covenant.

Keep reading!

DAY 24

THE BIG HEART

[Scheduled Reading: 1 Samuel 24 - 31]

The Bible might contain as much biographical data on David as it does for any other character.

Sure, Abraham has a nice portfolio of Bible space devoted to his life. So does Joseph and Moses. In the New Testament, Jesus and Paul have lots of print space.

But in terms of life events, family data, personal trials and triumph, thoughts and reflections, from teenager to adulthood to the deathbed - the biblical account of David is loaded (don't forget his many Psalms).

David's run from Saul is a dark season for him. Years of being essentially homeless – in the forests or in hide-out lands, dodging King Saul's armies.

David's two sneak attacks on Saul - and choosing to spare his life - show David's extreme discipline and willingness to further risk his own life to honor God.

Even David's men could not understand his logic for not killing Saul.

David's tenderness toward Saul and his family is exactly the kind of behavior that God found so appealing.

David's uniqueness was his heart. It's likely the reason for the lifetime of favor God heaped on this man.

It's the reason he was chosen king over Saul.

It's the reason for his many victories.

And I believe it's the reason for God's staggering covenant He made with David.

That's coming up tomorrow.

DAY 25

THE BIG PROMISE

[Scheduled Reading: 2 Samuel 1-8. Pay attention to Chapter 7.]

And your house and your kingdom shall be made sure forever before me. Your throne shall be established forever (2 Samuel 7:16).

God promised to establish David's throne FOREVER (2 Samuel 7:16).

That's BIG!

I'm not sure what David thought of this promise. Does anything on earth last forever?

Kingdoms rise and kingdoms fall. But forever is exactly what God had in mind.

God is talking about a Divine Kingdom.

To fast forward in our reading: 1,000 years after King David - and from the very line of David - Jesus (The SEED) will come to earth as the King of the Jews.

And one day still in the future, Jesus will resume his reign on earth and in the new heavens. And Christ will stand on the throne FOREVER.

Throughout the rest of the Bible, Jesus' name is closely connected to Abraham, Judah… and David.

If there was a Mount Rushmore for famous fathers of The Seed, it would have to include David!

Making Connections

Remember Jacob's blessing to Judah?

"The scepter shall not depart from Judah, nor the ruler's staff from between his feet, until tribute comes to him"

(Genesis 49:10).

Judah's blessing was the first hint that kings would come from his seed. Sure enough, David was that king.

Take a moment to review the Resets at page 28,

and note the Davidic Covenant.

DAY 26

THE BIG MESSY

[Scheduled Reading: 2 Samuel 9-16]

Just as everything in David's life was BIG, his sin was also BIG.

Sin is just messy.

His adultery with Bathsheba, and the cover-up by murdering her husband, left a sloppy mess for the rest of David's life.

God's judgment was direct.

His family would implode. His sons would be at war with each other. Some would even seek David's life. His wives would be captured and defiled by his enemies.

His baby born to Bathsheba died, too.

It was family dysfunction at its greatest. It was messy.

But something beautiful happens in this story - something that can be an encouragement to every one of us.

David repented BIG. He said to the prophet Nathan, "I have sinned against the Lord."

God's response should give us all goose bumps.

Nathan told David, "The Lord also has put away your sin."

As messy as it might be, forgiveness can be instant. Restoration can be immediate it. It was for King David.

That does not mean the consequences go away. Again, sin leaves behind a mess.

But past sin need not be a ball and chain tied to your ankle. Forgiveness is the weapon against sin.

Perhaps David's greatest life victory might not even be his fight against Goliath, or the Philistines, etc.

His greatest victory just might be his ability to repent and recover from his big sin.

David's fickle faith story is different than most.

Yes, he became content. He got distracted. He slipped into sin.

But he bounced back fast.

For the rest of David's life, he will wade through the fall-out of his BIG sin.

But because of his BIG heart, his walk with God does not suffer – instead it thrives.

DAY 27

FAMILY PROBLEMS

[Scheduled Reading: 2 Samuel 17-24]

David had several wives and nearly twenty sons.

Blended families with lots of wives can be complicated. And the fall-out from David's sin makes it extra messy.

Sibling rivalry is intense.

Brother rapes sister (Amnon & Tamar). Brother kills a brother (Absalom & Amnon) for revenge.

Son seeks father's life and dies in his pursuit to kill father (Absalom & David).

Sons jockey for authority (Adonijah & Solomon - see 1 Kings Chapter 1).

Let's step back and look at the big picture.

A son from this dysfunctional family is going to carry forward The Seed. Which son does God choose?

(Remember, we know that David's throne is going to endure forever. That's God's promise.)

Answer: God elects an offspring of Bathsheba, the woman with whom David committed his infamous adultery.

You'll recall the baby conceived out of David's adultery with Bathsheba did not live. But after Bathsheba's husband died at battle (orchestrated by David), she became David's wife and together they conceived another child...Solomon.

The Lord shows a special love for Solomon (2 Samuel 12:25).

The favor God shows for Solomon is about to get even BIGGER than the favor God showed David.

*Then David comforted his wife, Bathsheba, and went in to her and lay with her, and she bore a son, and he called his name **Solomon**. And the Lord loved him[25] and sent a message by Nathan the prophet. So he called his name Jedidiah, because of the Lord. 2 Samuel 12:24-25*

DAY 28

BIGGER

[Scheduled Reading: 1 Kings 1-5; 8-10]

King David's BIG legacy continues through his son Solomon. In fact, the story gets even BIGGER.

David must have taught his son to think BIG. And more importantly, to pray BIG (1 Kings 3).

In response to a BIG dream, a BIG offer, and a BIG ask, God gave Solomon wisdom and wealth in unprecedented proportions.

People were fascinated by this young man's expansive knowledge. He spoke 3,000 proverbs and was credited with 1,005 songs. He was an authority on animals, birds, reptiles, fish and trees.

His balance sheet was BIG. His assets included crazy amounts of gold and silver, and 40,000 stalls of horses and 12,000 horsemen, just to name a few select items.

His annual income included roughly 50,000 pounds of gold!

Solomon built a BIG temple for God (7-year project) and then a BIG house to live in (13-year project).

Meanwhile Israel enjoyed great peace and prosperity.

Dignitaries from all across the earth (i.e. the Queen of Sheba) paid visit to Solomon to witness his splendor.

From God's perspective, Solomon's kingdom made a statement to the world. It was an impressive symbol of God's favor and protection of the Israelite nation.

Despite this enormous kingdom position, something sad is about to happen.

A BIG fall.

Talk about it.

1 Kings 10 marks the high point of Israel's history.

For the rest of our Old Testament reading, Israel will be either in decline (or recovery).

You can make a mark in your Bible (with a pen or pencil or a sticky note) to mark this turning point in Israel's history.

Just as the Bible is divided by Old and New Testaments, 1 Kings 10 can be considered the division point between the good fortune (under David and Solomon) and the misfortune for the nation of Israel.

DAY 29

THE BIG 'IF'

[Scheduled Reading: 1 Kings 11]

Today's reading is just one single chapter - 1 Kings 11. The story of Israel is getting ready to experience a stunning reversal of fortune.

God gave Solomon wisdom, wealth and kingdom rule unlike ever seen on earth.

During Solomon's reign, God visited him in a dream for a second time and affirmed the Davidic promise to Solomon - that David's kingdom would endure forever (see 1 Kings 9).

But there was a big "IF" attached.

IF Solomon served and obeyed God, his kingdom would endure. But IF he turned from God, Israel would be torn from its land and the famous temple would be demolished.

Look back at 1 Kings 9 and notice the big "IF's":

⁴And as for you, if you will walk before me, as David your father walked, with integrity of heart and uprightness, doing according to all that I have commanded you, and keeping my statutes and my rules, ⁵ then I will establish your royal throne over Israel forever, as I promised David your father, saying, 'You shall not lack a man on the throne of Israel.'

⁶ But if you turn aside from following me, you or your children, and do not keep my commandments and my statutes that I have set before you, but go and serve other gods and worship them, ⁷ then I will cut off Israel from the land that I have given them, and the house that I have consecrated for my name I will cast out of my sight, and Israel will become a proverb and a by-word among all peoples. ⁸ And this house will become a heap of ruins. (1 Kings 9:4-8.)

Tragically, Solomon failed the test. He chose the 2nd of the Big "IF's."

Even in all his vast wisdom, he made devastating choices and turned away from God and toward the gods of his foreign wives.

God initiated Israel's decline and removed His hand of favor and prosperity from Israel.

Israel's decline is one of the saddest reversals in biblical history. And it was triggered by Solomon's walk-away from God.

Do you remember my call-out chapters from Leviticus 26 and Deuteronomy 28?

God warned the Israelites that his blessings were conditional. If God's children obey – they can expect prosperity. If they disobey God – curses.

Solomon's downfall was a direct outcome of this working conditional promise for the children of Israel.

Shocking…stunning…sad.

DAY 30

SOAKING IT IN

[Scheduled Reading: 1 Kings 11 continued]

We're at the middle of our 60-day reading journey.

It's a good day to take another pause from the reading plan (or catch up) and reflect on this change of fortune for Israel.

Centuries of forward progress (for Israel) are reversed in a single generation.

From Abraham, to Isaac, to Jacob... and all the way to King Solomon – was fifteen generations of fathers in the line of The Seed. The era covered roughly one thousand years.

Aside from the usual fickle-faith hiccups in the journey, things seemed to be working for The Seed.

During this millennial season, The Seed:

- departed from Ur and settled in Canaan (Abram),

- journeyed to Egypt to escape famine (Jacob),

- escaped from slavery back out of Egypt (led by Moses),

- entered the Promised Land (led by Joshua).

Along the way The Seed went from a small family, to a large family, to a collection of tribes, to a mighty nation.

As The Seed attained kingdom status, it achieved military dominance (under David) and ultimately world-renowned wealth and prosperity (under Solomon).

Next, The Seed begins a new trajectory - back to the bottom.

Just one man (King Solomon) triggers its downfall. God sets this fall in motion during Rehoboam's reign.

Rehoboam (#35) was Solomon's son – and next in the line of The Seed.

Here's how the kingdom collapse unfolds in 1 Kings 11.

1. God tells Solomon his kingdom will be torn apart.
2. It will happen during Rehoboam's reign.
3. God affirms His covenant with David and promises to leave one tribe with Rehoboam.

Any idea which tribe would stay with Solomon and Rehoboam's seed?

Answer: Judah!

God always has a plan to keep The Seed alive, right?

Bible Reading Hints

Bible-reading gets confusing throughout Kings (and Chronicles). Here's a tip. Israel split into two kingdoms:

-        *the ten northern tribes (called "Israel" in Samaria)*

-        *and two southern tribes (called "Judah" in Jerusalem).*

[Note: the tribe of Benjamin stays with Judah.]

The two initial kings are Jeroboam (Israel) and Rehoboam (Judah). That's another challenge- names start to run together.

Throughout the rest of Kings, the author bounces back and forth between the accounts of kings in Judah and Israel.

Day 31

IN GOD'S SIGHT

[Scheduled Reading: 1 Kings 12-18]

The next sixteen fathers in line of The Seed (Judah) are kings.

From the reign of Rehoboam when the kingdoms split, the kingdom of Judah lasts for just over three hundred fifty years (and roughly two hundred years for Israel).

Judah is led by mostly evil kings, with occasional good kings.

Remember the illustration of the western movies – the good guys and bad guys?

Well, now the cast in the line of The Seed gets a bit confusing.

Every member in the line of The Seed is a "good guy" in that they play a part in God's plan to transfer The Seed.

But when it comes to their character and behavior – they are far from good. Some not only are bad… they're wicked!

From God's perspective, these kings either "did right in the sight of the Lord" or "did evil in the sight of the Lord."

That's pretty much the summary judgment for each of Judah's kings. (For Israel, all of the kings are evil).

Most of the time God deals with kings and their respective kingdoms according to what their behavior deserves.

He intercedes for the righteous and inflicts judgment on the evil. Pretty straightforward.

To kick off this decline, God says to Rehoboam, "You have abandoned me, so I have abandoned you."

Sure enough, Jerusalem is plundered by the Egyptians.

Occasionally God's judgment seems delayed or absent.

Abijah (#36) follows the pattern (evil) of his father Rehoboam, but he has success against his adversaries.

Next we have **Asa (#37)** and **Jehoshaphat (#38)** – both righteous kings.

Both tear down the altars for idol worship and initiate worship reforms according to the law of Moses.

God honors both kings and gives them success against their enemies.

Reading through the books of Kings (and 2 Chronicles) can be tough reading. Times are dark and evil prevails.

The path of The Seed seems headed toward extinction at times. But as has been since the beginning, God is in control.

DAY 32

THE END IN MIND

[Scheduled Reading: 1 Kings 19 - 2 Kings 3]

The books of 1 & 2 Kings are difficult books for Bible readers.

Reading bounces around from king to king (mostly bad ones), and back and forth between the Judah (the two southern tribes) and Israel (the 10 northern tribes), all while tripping over difficult-to-remember names and depressing themes.

Focus is hard.

Sometimes the different kings from the two different kingdoms share the same name! (I know, doubly confusing!)

It helps to read these books with the end in mind – asking ourselves, "where are we headed?"

If you don't mind a little spoiler alert – lets talk about that.

Both the northern and southern tribes are headed toward exile.

Remember, that's the path initiated by Solomon's sad departure from God.

While 1 & 2 Kings (and 2 Chronicles) cover history for both kingdoms, extra attention focuses on Judah.

That makes perfect sense because Judah carries The Seed.

It also makes sense that the transfer of power for Judah stays on track within the family line, while power transfer gets off track for Israel.

Why would this matter? Because God promised David that his throne (and effectively his seed) would endure forever. So God keeps the path of The Seed intact for Judah.

But for Israel, the family line doesn't really matter, does it?

Israel will be conquered first. Every single one of Israel's kings were deemed "evil in the sight of the Lord", helping to move this northern kingdom "off the grid" sooner.

Meanwhile, Judah will last a little while longer. The occasional righteous kings, balanced with the mostly evil kings, help to slow the race toward exile.

Like I said. This is very tough reading.

Sometimes knowing the big picture and the down-the-line story points can take the pressure away from trying to understand everything.

DAY 33

CLOSE CALLS

[Scheduled Reading: 2 Kings 4-11]

It's a dismal decline for Judah. Fending off enemies, fighting with Israel, conspiracies, assassinations, take-over attempts.

Business as usual for power-hungry, fear-driven monarchies.

Amazingly, the transfer of The Seed is never disrupted.

After Asa and Jehoshaphat (good kings), **Joram (#39)** succeeds the throne. He resumes the wicked ways of his great grandfather, Abijah. He kills his six brothers (yes, those are Jehoshaphat's sons!)

Despite this atrocity, the Lord is not willing to destroy Judah because of His covenant with David (2 Chronicles 21:7).

God continues to have His way with the path of The Seed – seeking to fulfill His covenants and Genesis 3:15 promise.

After all, these men (even the most wicked ones) are ancestors to Jesus!

Unlike in the north (Israel) where kings bounce around from tribe to tribe, southern kingdom rule stays with the tribe of Judah.

And while family succession for Israel occasionally hits a dead end - with no son to succeed the throne - Judah always seems to find a way to pass The Seed. We're learning to expect that with God's Seed Strategy, right?

There are some close calls, though.

For example, **Ahaziah (#40**, son of Joram) reigns for a single year, before being assassinated by the king of Israel.

This assassination was ordained by God. (Just because Ahaziah was in the line of The Seed, did not guarantee God's protection.)

Then Ahaziah's mother, Athaliah, kills the remainder of the royal family - including Ahaziah's sons! (Yes, she murders her grand-babies!)

But what about The Seed?

As God's sovereignty would have it, Ahaziah's sister rescues Ahaziah's one-year old son, baby **Joash (#41),** and steals him away. She hides the baby Joash in the temple for six years while Athaliah is ruling as queen!

Queen Athaliah is eventually assassinated by a priest (another God-orchestrated death). And Joash assumes the throne as a seven-year-old kid!

Unbelievable! That's called protecting The Seed!

Joash goes on to be a good king – "doing what was right in the sight of the Lord." But his righteousness did fade toward the end of his 40-year reign.

It's hard to remain faithful to God when times are dark.

Lets talk about it.

The Seed is locked in a fierce battle with Satan.

Can you imagine what a victory it would be for Satan to work out the death of a king in line of The Seed?

Discuss how miraculous it is that God continues to keep The Seed safe and alive during this period of kingdom decline.

Day 34

EXILE UP NORTH

[Scheduled Reading: 2 Kings 12-17]

Joash's son **Amaziah (#42)** follows a similar path. He starts off with a "good king" legacy. But he too turns away from God later in life.

(Notice the pattern of many kings – start good, finish bad.)

Next in line of The Seed is **Azariah (#43 a.k.a. Uzziah)** and **Jotham (#44)**. Both are "mostly good" kings.

Meanwhile, something sad is about to happen up north for Israel.

After nineteen straight evil kings, Israel is invaded by Assyria. Its people are deported, bringing the end to the ten northern tribes.

They scatter and never return to their identity as individual tribes or even as a kingdom.

Meanwhile Judah's captivity is coming soon, too. It is roughly one hundred fifty years away. They will also be exiled… but God has a plan for their eventual return.

And why does God plan a return for Judah and not for Israel?

Of course… The Seed.

DAY 35

INTERMISSION

[Scheduled Reading: 2 Kings 18-25]

The erratic see-sawing of good kings and bad kings continues for Judah.

After Azzariah and Jotham (both good kings), the next king, **Ahaz (#45),** sinks Judah into deeper darkness. Among his notables is sacrificing his sons in the fire to the idol Molech!

Shockingly, somehow Ahaz's son, **Hezekiah (#46)**, grows up to be a great God-fearing king. (Think about it, Hezekiah's very own brothers are sacrificed by their father Ahaz!)

Hezekiah seeks to undo the sins of Ahaz and labors dutifully to restore worship reforms for Judah.

As the see-saw motion goes, Hezekiah is succeeded by King **Manasseh (#47)** who also burns his son as an offering.

It's amazing that these children-sacrificing kings do not extinguish The Seed along the way! (Of course, God would prevent that wouldn't He?)

After another evil king, **Amon (#48)**, Judah claims another legendary God-fearing king, **Josiah (#49)**.

Josiah discovered the Books of the Law and once again restores the worship customs, feasts and sacrifices for Judah.

Let's go back to King Hezekiah for a moment. There's a significant prophecy given to him.

The prophet Isaiah tells Hezekiah that a day is coming when all the kingdom treasures, and even the kings sons, will be

carried off to Babylon. (2 Kings 20:16-19)

Yes, Babylon!

If God wants to expose the people for their sins and humble them to their knees, I think exile to Babylon might do it.

Remember, God led Abraham away from Ur (nearby Babylon) and toward an open spacious land so that the Seed Family could grow and thrive. **Going back to Babylon is nearly fifteen hundred (1,500) years backwards!**

Sure enough, King Nebuchadnezzar of Babylon invades Jerusalem and captures **King Jehoiakim (#50).**

Later Nebuchadnezzar invades again and this time carries off Jehoiakim's son, **King Jeconiah (#51)**, the royal family, all the royal treasures and the remainder of the inhabitants of Jerusalem (leaving behind only the poorest of the land).

Roughly ten years later (587 BC), Babylon returns and Jerusalem is finally, fully desolated and officially in exile.

There's supposed to be a special SEED, a baby boy, born in nearby Bethlehem in about 590 years. But The Seed is stuck in Babylon!

If we were watching this Bible reading journey as a play, now might be a good time for intermission. How about a popcorn break?

Talk about it

Does it surprise you to see how God allows the Israelite nation to crumble and fall into complete disarray and captivity?

Why or why not?

DAY 36

SEED OF BABYLON

[Scheduled Reading: Ezra 1-8]

The books of Ezra and Nehemiah are significant turning points for The Seed. After a 70-year exile in Babylon, God opens the door for a return to Jerusalem. Notice how God accomplishes this.

He turns bad guys into good guys.

Babylonian leaders Cyrus and Darius become God's instruments to send groups of exiled Israelites back to Jerusalem.
So instead of playing "bad guy" roles (this is Babylon, right!), they're "good guys" helping The Seed get back on track.

This is another example of how God gets done what He wants done. And He'll even use the enemy to do it!

Ezra and Nehemiah are the famous "Good Guys."

They both lead a company of men back to Jerusalem to rebuild the temple and walls and restore worship for Judah.
When we think of the rebuilding projects, we mostly think of Ezra and Nehemiah. Their names get the most press.

But the first one to lead a mission trip back to Jerusalem was not Ezra or Nehemiah. It was a man named Zerubbabel (Ezra 2:2).

"And who is Zerubbabel?" you ask. He's a descendant of David - and the one who will carry The Seed forward. (You'll find his name sprinkled nine times throughout Ezra and Nehemiah.

Can you find them :)

Zerubbabel is a mostly <u>un-familiar</u> name in the line of The Seed.

But his legacy is ginormous! And guess what *Zerubbabel* means? *Answer: "The Seed of Babylon."*

Zerubbabel (#52), son of **Shealtiel (#51)**, was born in Babylon during Judah's exile! (Zerubbabel was grandson to the rotten King Jechoniah.)

The father-son combo, *"Zerubbabel, son of Shealtiel"* is referenced nearly a dozen times throughout the books of Ezra, Nehemiah and Haggai.

Zerubbabel finds favor during Judah's exile and is positioned as governor of Judah. Zerubbabel not only falls in line of The Seed – but he's also in a line of history's famous travelers who help to transport The Seed during various pivot points.

- Abraham transported The Seed from Ur to Haran to Canaan.

- Joseph paved the way to escape famine in Canaan to Egypt.

- Later Moses rescued The Seed from Egyptian slavery.

- After an unexpected detour to Babylon, God used Zerubbabel to get The Seed back to Jerusalem.

The Seed is going back home to Jerusalem. And Zerubbabel leads the way.

Tracking The Seed

If you've not done so in a while, take the time to update

The Seed Chart through today's reading.

Again, Zerubbabel is # 52!

DAY 37

REBUILDING WORSHIP

[Scheduled Reading: Ezra 9-10, Nehemiah 1-6]

While Ezra and Nehemiah are rebuilding temples and walls, they're also rebuilding something else.

Worship.

Upon their return from 70-year exile in Babylon, among the first orders of business is to build the altar (Ezra 3).

Why the altar?

Sacrifices!

Eventually the Israelites hold the first Passover celebration in over a few centuries.

They gather and organize the Levites to restore Jerusalem to working order.

Rebuilding Jerusalem means reigniting worship. And igniting worship means preparing hearts.

That's right. Worship is not just something we do to go through the motions. Worship involves our hearts.

Both Ezra and Nehemiah work to bring about heart healing by dealing with various sins among the Israelite community.

Intermarriage is a problem (Ezra 9 & 10, Nehemiah 13). Nehemiah reminds them that the very downfall of Israel was triggered by Solomon's intermarriage and infiltration of foreign gods.

Another problem is the oppression against the poor among them (Nehemiah 5).

Both men lead the people through a healthy process of confessing sins (Ezra 10, Nehemiah 9).

We're talking prayer-fasted, bitter-weeping, sack-cloth-wearing children throwing themselves down on their knees before God.

It's a total clean out – from the heart.

There's one more critical reform that both Ezra and Nehemiah institute.

I'll save that for tomorrow.

DAY 38

POWER READING

[Scheduled Reading: Nehemiah 7-13]

Ezra and Nehemiah institute something very special for the Israelites upon their return to Jerusalem.

Power Reading.

That's right.

Power Reading the Bible has been around for a long time.

Ezra was a scribe and he loved to teach. He knew the power and the value of God's holy word.

Ezra would read the word of God to a public assembly of people. He stood on a wooden platform and read from "early morning until midday, in the presence of the men and the women of those who could understand" (Nehemiah 8:3).

As he read the law the people wept. Most of them had never heard these words.

During the Feast of Booths celebration, starting on the first day of the month he read daily for seven straight days. *And day by day, from the first day to the last day, he read from the Book of the Law of God. (Nehemiah 8:18)*

Again, that's seven days of power reading the Bible, listening to God's Word read from early in the morning till midday!

Get this – on the 24th day of the month they're still meeting… and power reading! (Neh. 9:1).

And they read from the Book of the Law for a quarter of the day! (v3)

And for another quarter of the day they make confession and worship God.

I'm not sure if a "quarter of a day" is six hours of a 24-hour day or three hours of a half day, etc.? Still, we get the idea, don't we?

This has me asking myself, when's the last time I did anything for a quarter of the day (besides watching football)?

This should encourage all of us Power Readers!

Volume Bible consumption is what you do when you're going through spiritual renewal and seasons of revival.

Reading God's word for hours at a time is what you do to rebuild a heart for worship.

Talk Time

How has your Bible reading routine been going for you over the past several weeks? What benefits or takeaways can you share about being in God's Word on a regular basis?

DAY 39

ROCK STARS

[Scheduled Reading: Isaiah 1-9]

During Israel's decline, the real Bible rock stars are not the kings. They are the prophets!

These prophets are not in the line of The Seed. Most are not even from the tribe of Judah (Daniel was an exception).

Their role is to tell the kings what God is planning to do.

The kings are mostly unreceptive and threaten to kill the prophets. Many prophets die gruesome deaths at the hands of wicked kings.

The words of the Prophets are spoken during the 500 years of Israel's decline (after King David to their exile).

Chronologically, the accounts of these 17 books (5 major prophets and 12 minor prophets) coincide with the books of Kings and Chronicles.

While most of the prophet writings are not in this reading plan, I have selected a few portions to help us make some key connections.

The book of Isaiah kicks off the prophet writings.

You may remember earlier in our reading, the prophet Isaiah tells Hezekiah (one of the good kings) that a day is coming when all the kingdom treasures, and even the kings sons, would be carried off to Babylon. (2 Kings 20:16-19)

Sure enough, that happens.

Isaiah makes another stunning prophecy about the remnant that would return to Jerusalem (with Zerubbabel, Ezra and Nehemiah).

If the Lord of hosts had not left us a few survivors, we should have been like Sodom, and become like Gomorrah. Isaiah 1:9

Bible historians consider Isaiah to be the prophet who understood the most about the coming Messiah – The Seed.

Isaiah Chapter 9 speaks to this foreknowledge:

For to us a child is born, to us a son is given; and the government shall be upon his shoulder, and his name shall be called Wonderful Counselor, Mighty God, Everlasting Father, Prince of Peace.

Of the increase of his government and of peace, there will be no end, on the throne of David and over his kingdom, to establish it and to uphold it with justice and with righteousness from this time forth and forevermore. (Isaiah 9:6-7).

Isaiah knew where things were headed. A SEED from the line of David will come and rule forever.

That's where things are headed in this Bible read.

Continue on, friends.

DAY 40

DIRTY JOBS

[Scheduled Reading: Jeremiah 18-25]

There was a TV show called *Dirty Jobs* where host Mike Rowe took on the most difficult, strange, disgusting, or messy occupational duties.

When I think of the biblical prophets, I think of the ultimate "dirty jobs."

As mentioned yesterday, prophet work was downright dangerous...even deadly.

Check out the fate of some of the prophets:
➢ Isaiah suffered martyrdom by being sawn in two by King Manasseh (and Manasseh is in the line of Christ!)
➢ Jeremiah suffered martyrdom by stoning at Tahpanhes in Ancient Egypt
➢ Ezekiel suffered martyrdom in the land of the Chaldeans
➢ Some of the minor prophets were martyred as well (i.e. Micah, Amos)

These Prophets were special men and a special resurrection awaits them one day.

Back to our prophet discussions, I want to focus on Jeremiah's prophecy in Chapter 25.

God has some special events planned.

- Judah will be captured by Babylon and exiled from their land. *[check – that happens]*

- Babylonian captivity will last 70 years. *[check – that happens, too]*

- After 70 years, God will bring judgment on Babylon, conquered by Cyrus the Great of the Persian Empire. *[check, another fulfillment]*

- A remnant of Judah will return to Jerusalem. *[check again]*

Wow, this is exactly what happens, isn't it?

We read about Babylonian exile at the end of 2 Kings. Then we read about the remnant return to Jerusalem in Ezra & Nehemiah.

Isn't it fascinating how God works through the Babylonians?

Babylon (bad guys) takes over the good guys (Israelites), then God brings along other bad guys (Cyrus of Persia) to punish Babylon!

Then God works through Cyrus to show favor on the exiled Israelites.

God's sovereignty is stunning.

DAY 41

CONTEXT MATTERS

[Scheduled Reading: Jeremiah 26-34]

One of the cool experiences about power-reading through the Bible is the opportunity to gain context.

While cruising through Jeremiah you'll encounter a familiar passage:

For I know the plans I have for you, declares the Lord, plans for welfare and not for evil, to give you a future and a hope (Jer. 29:11).

It's one of the most famous and frequently quoted verses in the Bible. But most Christians don't know the context of this passage.

For 41 days we've been reading about the Journey of The Seed: starting with Adam… and eventually Noah… then Abraham…. then King David…

After the kingdom divides (the southern and northern split), and after both kingdoms are captured, **God wants His children to know He has their future in His control.**

God wants the Israelites to know that after 70 years of exile are complete, they will be restored to their rightful place in Jerusalem.

Sure enough, this happens through Zerubbabel, Ezra and Nehemiah.

Understanding the Bible's big-picture helps to understand the context of the prophets!

Day 42

DANIEL…A SPECIAL MAN

[Scheduled Reading: Daniel 1-6]

Growing up, Daniel was one of my favorite Bible figures.

The book of Daniel contains many of the famous Bible stories that are taught to children...the fiery furnace, the handwriting on the wall, Daniel in the lion's den, Nebuchadnezzar's famous dreams.

He's still among my favorites. He must be one of God's favorites, too (check out Ezekiel 14:14 & 20.)

Seriously though, I don't want to speculate on God having favorite kids. But you have to admit – those verses in Ezekiel are pretty cool.

Daniel is one of the few prophets who comes from the line of Judah. He was among the royal family and in the first group to be exiled during Babylon's initial breach against Judah.

Daniel was sharp – he understood Bible history. Of course they didn't call it "Bible history". But he understood the significance of the legacy of The Seed through David and Judah.

He likely had an idea of what was going on. While we have the benefit of history and are studying the Bible's big picture from the rearview mirror, Daniel was in the midst of it all.

Exiled from Jerusalem – Daniel was raised in Babylon, learning the Babylonian culture.

Daniel finds himself interpreting a series of dreams for the Babylon's ruler, and later interprets a strange handwriting on the wall incident.

And what exactly was the message God had for the Babylonian king (Belshazzar)?

That the Babylonian kingdom was getting ready to end.

Sure enough, Belshazzar is killed that very night. And the kingdom is wrestled away from Babylon and seized by the Medes and Persians.

Yep – the Medes and Persians are the ones God uses to send the tribe of Judah back to Jerusalem.

Daniel has a fascinating position in Bible history.

- He lived in Jerusalem before exile.

- He lived in Babylon during exile.

- Then he witnesses the downfall of Babylon and likely witnessed the return of the remnant to Jerusalem.

Guess what now?

We're at the end of our Old Testament Reading.

Time to Talk

What are some of your reactions and reflections after completing the Old Testament reading?

What themes stands out most to you?

DAY 43

SEVENTH INNING STRETCH

[Scheduled Reading: Free/Catch-up Day]

Congratulations! You've finished the Old Testament section of the reading plan.

Use this day to catch-up if needed, or just take a reading break.

If you've been to a nine-inning baseball game – you might be familiar with the seventh-inning stretch.

It's when the crowd stands up to stretch their legs and shake their arms before sitting back down.

That's sort of where we're at in our reading – we're beginning the seventh week, with just over two weeks remaining.

We've covered four thousand years of biblical history in our reading so far.

God is taking His time routing The Seed through human history.

And we're about to arrive at a major destination… but not the final destination.

The arrival of The Seed is right around the corner!

DAY 44

SILENT NIGHTS

[Scheduled Reading: Matthew 1-4]

After the prophet Malachi, there were roughly 400 years of silent nights.

I'm talking about the roughly 146,000 days of silence from God.

There are no biblical accounts to report between the book of Malachi and the four gospel accounts (Matthew, Mark, Luke and John) - between the Old and New Testaments.

No prophet stirrings. No angel appearances. Nothing.

But guess what? Bible genealogies do give us some nuggets from this era. The Seed carriers!

Check it out below:

*And after the deportation to Babylon: Jechoniah was the father of Shealtiel, and Shealtiel the father of Zerubbabel, and Zerubbabel the father of **Abiud**, and Abiud the father of **Eliakim**, and Eliakim the father of **Azor**, and Azor the father of **Zadok**, and Zadok the father of **Achim**, and Achim the father of **Eliud**, and Eliud the father of **Eleazar**, and Eleazar the father of **Matthan**, and Matthan the father of **Jacob**, and Jacob the father of **Joseph** the husband of Mary, of whom **Jesus** was born, who is called Christ. (Matthew 1:12-16)*

How special is it to know that the only mention of the 400-year silence is the fathers in line of The Seed!

Matthew's genealogy mentions nine fathers that carry The Seed forward from Zerubbabel (#53).

Abiud (#54), Eliakim (#55), Azor (#56), Sadoc (#57), Achim (#58), Eliud (#59), Eleazar (#60), Matthan (#61), Jacob (#62).

We know nothing else about these men.

The fact that we have their names says something about God's desire for us to have this precious Seed history.

Of course we know the tenth father mentioned – **Joseph**, husband to Mary. He's **#63** in the line of The Seed!

And finally, there's **#64, The SEED. Jesus Christ!**

For 42 days we've been reading through the Old Testament.

Finally we arrive at The SEED from Genesis 3:15. The seed of the woman. The Christ child. The Messiah.

Matthew makes helpful connections to the Old Testament. If you're reading Matthew 1-4 from a Bible with references, you'll notice the links to the various prophets (Isaiah, Micah, Jeremiah, Hosea).

Even the account of Jesus being tempted by Satan (Matt. 4:4, 6, 7, 10) contains references Jesus makes to Old Testament texts (Deuteronomy and Psalms).

Reading the New Testament can feel like reading a completely different Bible. But the links to the Old Testament show us how interconnected this Bible's story really is.

Tracking The Seed

Take the time to update The Seed Chart all the way to

Jesus Christ.

DAY 45

LINE OF KINGS

[Scheduled Reading: Luke 1-3]

Each of the gospel writers gives us a different look at The Seed.

In Luke 3 we see another genealogy. If you look closely you'll notice different names of certain fathers compared to Matthew's genealogy.

Actually it looks like a completely different genealogy. Why is that?

Matthew presents the ancestry of The Seed through Joseph (stepfather to Jesus).

Luke traces the ancestry of The Seed through the mother Mary.

Both Mary and Joseph trace their lineage to King David, tribe of Judah.

But Joseph's line traces to King Solomon while Mary's line traces to another of David's sons, Nathan.

So why does Joseph come from a line of kings and Mary does not? After all – Mary is the birth mother. (And Joseph might be considered a stepfather.)

This is a weighty question and plenty of scholarly work has been devoted to this matter – the short answer is this.

Under Jewish history, family genealogy follows the line of the father. Joseph was the legal father (or guardian) to Jesus.

The reason Jesus was born in Bethlehem is because Joseph had returned to his hometown to be registered for the mandatory census.

Joseph is from Bethlehem, from the line of Kings. Jesus is the king of the Jews in the line of Joseph.

Fascinating!

DAY 46

THE SEED IS GOD

[Scheduled Reading: John 1-7]

For us Bible readers, another gospel account means another perspective of The Seed.

While the gospel accounts of Matthew and Luke present the genealogies of Joseph and Mary, John focuses on Jesus' deity.

In the beginning was the Word and the Word was with God and the Word was God. He was in the beginning with God... And the Word became flesh and dwelt among us. (John 1:1-2, 14)

Sounds like a tongue twister, doesn't it?

Jesus is God. The SEED is God.

It's a mind-boggling idea. The trinity is not easy to grasp. It's what makes the Christian faith so unique.

John summarizes the full gospel message right away.
But to all... who believed in his name, he gave the right to become children of God (v12).

This is a working premise throughout the book of John. Those who believe in this SEED, Christ Jesus, can become children of God and have eternal life.

For God so loved the world, that he gave his only Son, that whoever believes in him should not perish but have eternal life (v3:16).

And how exactly did God give Jesus to the world?

As a sacrifice.

This leads us to another significant description of Jesus. Jesus is the Passover Lamb.

"Behold the Lamb of God, who takes away the sin of the world!" (1:28).

The SEED is God. And The SEED is a Lamb.

Hang on to this thought. This will have special meaning for us in the days ahead.

DAY 47

HOLY WEEK

[Scheduled Reading: John 8-14]

Much of the book of John covers roughly a single week of history.

Today we call it Holy Week. It's the week before Easter.

Let's look at what typically occurred during Holy week, beginning on the 10th day of the first month of the year.

- On the 10th day, five days before Passover, a lamb was selected for sacrifice.
- For the next four days, the lamb was observed. It was to be a perfect male lamb.
- Finally on Passover Day, the lamb was sacrificed.

On this particular Passover week, Jesus comes on the scene as the Passover Lamb and goes through a similar routine as the barnyard lamb.

- Five days before Passover, Jesus rides into Bethany on a donkey. [The Lamb is selected.]
- For the next four days, Jesus is questioned by the religious authorities. [The Lamb is inspected]
- On Passover, Jesus is sacrificed. [The Lamb is sacrificed.]

Something else happened on this Passover week. Three days later, Jesus was resurrected from the dead.

It's the most stunning single event in history.

This makes for a historic Holy week.

As you read the book of John, be sure to take notice of various mentions of this Passover week:

- John 11:55 and 12:1 – "six days before the Passover"

- John 12:12-15 – "the next day" Jesus rides on the donkey

- John 13:1 – before the Passover Feast

- John 19:14 – it was the day of Preparation of the Passover

- John 19:31 – it was the day of Preparation

Understanding the context of this historic holy week shines a different light on these passages in John's Gospel, doesn't it!

Seed Perspective

We're still reading, but The Seed Journey is complete.

How does reading the Bible from the "Seed Perspective"

change your view of the virgin birth and the story

of Mary and Joseph?

DAY 48

BIZARRE STORY

[Scheduled Reading: John 15-21]

Here's the gospel storyline, in a nutshell:

> ➤ After 4,000 years of biblical history, our God comes to earth as The SEED.

> ➤ He is born a baby.

> ➤ He grows up a man.

> ➤ He dies as a slaughtered lamb.

> ➤ After a brief return to earth, He goes back to heaven. (Acts 1)

At first glance, it's a bizarre story.

I recently read this quote: "Christianity is the only major religion to have as its central event the humiliation of its God." (*Church History* by Bruce Shelley).

But for those of us tracking the biblical narrative as part of this 60-day read, it makes sense.

For 4,000 years, God has been routing The Seed through history. Meanwhile, Satan seeks to destroy The Seed.

At every turn there's a threat. Even after Jesus was born, the King Herod sought to kill all baby boys. But God routed Joseph to escape to Egypt.

Finally, The SEED is killed. Surely Satan thought the battle was over.

Instead, Jesus came back to life.

Satan must have been stunned! The Seed he had fought so hard to extinguish – could not be destroyed.

It's been 2,000 years since that resurrection event.

The SEED lives on. But the battle is not over. Satan still has destructive powers and influence on earth.

But a day is coming in the future when the final blow will be delivered…

When The SEED will crush the head of the serpent, just as God promised in Genesis 3:15.

Let's Review the Bible's Big Picture

The Bible is about the journey of The Seed:

- that travels through 4,000 years,

- consisting of roughly 60+ generations,

- connected by six (6) key reset events,

*- **focused on two (2) resurrection events,***

- which set up one (1) climactic redemptive event: the recreation of the Heavens and the Earth.

We just covered the first of the two resurrection events. Everything so far is historical. The rest of the Bible's Big Picture is future events – prophecy.

DAY 49

ANOTHER PAUSE

[Scheduled Reading: Free/Catch-up Day]

Enjoy another pause from the reading plan today.

Here's where we are headed for the rest of the 60-day reading plan.

<u>Acts</u> – It's a continuation of the gospels. While the gospels report the history of the life of Christ, Acts contains the history of the early church.

<u>Hebrews</u> – This book helps make useful connections between the Old and New Testaments.

<u>Revelation</u> – I call this book the "Final Testament." There are the Old and New Testaments… and then Revelation, the Final Testament.

We're almost through our 60-day journey!

DAY 50

BIBLE HISTORY

[Scheduled Reading: Acts 1-7]

After his death and miraculous resurrection, Jesus ascends back to heaven.

The disciples watch as Jesus floats into the clouds. What an incredible sight!

So what happens next? Lots of preaching and evangelism.

The apostles are fired up and more committed than ever to spread the message of The Seed.

Peter preaches actively. A man named Stephen preaches. Paul comes along soon to preach.

And guess how these preachers preached?

By sharing Bible history!

Of course they didn't yet have the printed Bible collection that we have today. These preachers would have called it something different – maybe the "history of Christ… or the "history of Israel."

Anyway, that seemed to be the common method for evangelism - to share their history, connecting The SEED to their forefathers all the way back to Abraham.

Consider Stephen's famous speech (Acts Chapter 7) just before being stoned by the crowd.

The speech was nearly 1,300 words!

Stephen chronicles Abraham's journey from Ur to Haran, then to the present-day land of Israel.

He covers Isaac and Jacob...and Joseph.

Then Moses and Joshua... David and Solomon.

He covers 2,000 years of Bible history.

Stephen knew that the people likely knew their history, too.

But they didn't appreciate when Stephen suggested that it was their fathers who murdered the prophets... and murdered Jesus!

This made the crowds mad. They rushed toward Stephen and stoned him to death on the spot.

Stephen's final conversation before his death was sharing the history of Israel with the crowd that would eventually kill him.

If you want a refresher of the past 50 days of our Bible read, take special notice of Acts Chapter 7.

It's a great summary of Bible history.

DAY 51

ANOTHER STONING

[Scheduled Reading: Acts 8-14]

Guess who stood over the body of Stephen to witness and sign off on Stephen's execution? A man named Saul.

Ironically, Saul went on to have his own conversion experience. He also received a new name, "Paul" (see Acts 9).

And in early church fashion, Paul went on to preach just like Stephen did... by sharing Bible history (see Acts 13:16-41).

Like Stephen, during one preaching session Paul shares the history of Israel: their escape from Egypt, the wilderness wanderings, entrance into the Promised Land, the era of judges, the emergence of kings (Saul and David).

Like Stephen, Paul takes time to carefully connect Israel's history to the person of Jesus Christ.

Some days after his speech, guess what happens to Paul?

He is stoned! Yes, just like Stephen.

The people left him for dead, but he miraculously stands up to his feet and resumes preaching the very next day (Acts 14:19-20).

There's a frightening pattern throughout the book of Acts.

Godly men get fired up about The SEED and preach Bible history.

Evil men become angry at these words, and they kill the messengers.

This happens to Stephen. It almost happens to Paul.

It happens to James the brother of John who was killed by Herod the King (Acts 12:2).

During early church history, the fate of the disciples is similar to the Old Testament prophets.

Spreading the truth about the history of The SEED was costly!

Family Talk

Take time as a family to discuss Stephen (Acts 7) and Paul's (Acts 13) speech. What do you admire about his speech?

Have you had opportunity during this reading journey to discuss the Bible with someone else (either a believe or non-believer)? Share any experiences you may have had.

DAY 52

ACTS & THE EPISTLES

[Scheduled Reading: Acts 15-21]

The book of Acts simply reports the "acts of the apostles."

It's labeled as one of the Bible's "history" books, covering the launch of the early church.

Many of Paul's missionary journeys are reported in Acts. As he traveled to cities and visited churches, he wrote letters.

Many of these letters (or epistles) are included throughout the New Testament.

For example, Paul visited

- Thessalonica (Ch. 17) – see books of Thessalonians
- Corinth (Ch. 18) – see books of Corinthians
- Ephesus (Ch. 18 & 19) – see book of Ephesians
- Rome (Ch. 27 & 28) – see book of Romans

It is believed that Paul wrote at least 8 epistles and as many as 13 letters could be attributed to him.

To keep us focused on the Big Picture narrative of the Bible, I've excluded these letters from our 60-day journey.

Each of these epistles accomplishes similar goals. The chief goal is to share the mystery of The Seed - the life, sacrifice and resurrection of Jesus Christ.

In the first few verses of each epistle, Paul identifies himself as a "servant" or an "apostle" of Jesus Christ.

In your future Bible readings of these epistles (separate from this 60-day plan), notice Paul's many mentions of the name and person of Jesus Christ.

The Second Resurrection

One of Paul's teaching themes is the resurrection of the dead. This second resurrection (the first is that of Jesus Christ) is crucial to the Bible's Big Picture.

It's the reason that we have hope. Just as Christ was raised to life, those of us in Christ Jesus will one day experience a bodily resurrection and eternal life with God in heaven.

Here are some mentions of this resurrection: Daniel 12:2; Mark 12:24-27; John 5:28-29; Acts 24:15; 26:8; 1 Corinthians 15:12, 52; 1 Thessalonians 4:16; Revelation 20:12-13.

DAY 53

TESTIMONY POWER

[Scheduled Reading: Acts 22-28]

Apostle Paul was one sharp cookie.

He was extremely versed in the law of Judaism, educated by the famous Gamaliel.

He understood politics. And he understood the inner workings of the various legal systems and the interrelationship between various authorities (civic and religious).

Paul used this knowledge and expertise to his advantage.

Paul was arrested and jailed frequently, but he was hard to pin down because of his slippery ways.

Sometimes he wormed his way out of trouble by defending and claiming his unique legal and citizenship rights.

And other times he had the assistance of more divine escape measures – like when angels appeared during the night to walk him out of his cell.

But one of Paul's favorite responses was to share his personal testimony.

Paul had several opportunities to share his full story (chapter 22 & 26), as well as opportunities to reason with various authorities in attempt to share the gospel.

Apostle Paul's role in biblical history is legendary. He was among the most unlikely candidates to be chosen for his role.

Since Abraham, God's covenant relationship rested with the Israelite nation – the Jews.

But Paul was chosen as the evangelist to share the faith with the non-Jewish world.

His testimony was powerful. He was a Jew (from tribe of Benjamin) – but he once persecuted Christians to death.

His blinding light experience on the road to Damascus was the famous turning point – an encounter with Jesus.

This encounter opened up the Christian faith to the non-Jewish world. And since then, the gospel has been advancing forcefully.

Thanks to a man named Paul and his powerful testimony.

But the Lord said to him, "Go, for he is a chosen instrument of mine to carry my name before the Gentiles and Kings and the children of Israel. For I will show him how much he must suffer for the sake of my name." Acts 9:15-16

Family Talk

Have you taken time to craft your own personal testimony?

Practice sharing your faith story/testimony with your family. Consider (a) when and how you came to know Jesus? (b) what it is that you believe about him? (c) and why?

DAY 54

ROLES OF THE SEED

[Scheduled Reading: Hebrews 1-7]

The book of Hebrews seems mostly focused on Jesus Christ...
The SEED.

The author (unknown) takes time to celebrate Jesus' unique roles.

- <u>Jesus is God's son (Ch. 1)</u>. He's the radiance of the glory of God and the exact imprint of his nature.

- <u>Jesus is greater than angels (Ch. 1 & 2)</u>. This seems like a no-brainer to us, but angels have always been special. Angels are considered "sons of God", just as Jesus is a son of God. But of course, Jesus is much greater.

- <u>Jesus is human, of flesh and blood (Ch. 2).</u> He was made like his brother (us) so that he could suffer for us.

- <u>Jesus is greater than Moses (Ch. 3)</u>. Again, another no-brainer to us. But to early Christians, Moses' role and favor with God was legendary.

- <u>Jesus is the Great High Priest (Ch. 4, 5, 7 & 8)</u>, offering up a sacrifice for sins.

- <u>Jesus is the final sacrifice (Ch. 10)</u>, brining to end the era of animal sacrifices.

Hebrews is a book that should be studied. It's a tough book to just read casually or in a "Power Read" manner.

Recently I listened to the book repeatedly, over a half dozen times in a week-long period, seeking to become more familiar with its teachings.

For New Testament readers seeking to understand the deep symbolism of Jesus Christ, the book of Hebrews is a treasure.

DAY 55

A CLOUD OF WITNESSES

[Scheduled Reading: Hebrews 8-13]

As we are learning, history is important to the New Testament writers.

Consider, Hebrews Chapter 11 - one of my favorite chapters in the Bible.

It's known as the "Faith Hall of Fame" chapter - a roll call of faith heroes who lived life looking ahead to a reward. A reward yet to be received when they died.

(That means they were looking forward to their reward in heaven.)

The roll call begins with Abel. Then Enoch, Noah, Abraham, Isaac and Jacob.

Joseph and Moses.

Rahab, Gideon, Barak, Samson, Jephthah, David and Samuel. Many unnamed heroes are mentioned as well.

Some of the unknown faith heroes endured extreme persecution and fatal outcomes in exchange for heavenly rewards.

They were stoned, they were sawn in two, they were killed with the sword (Hebrews 11:37).

Bible history is crucial!

It equips us with knowledge of the past. And offers heroes to encourage us as we walk into the future.
The Bible calls these heroes, our *witnesses*.

Therefore, since we are surrounded by so great a cloud of witnesses, let us also lay aside every weight , and the sin which clings so closely, and let us run with endurance the race that is set before us... (Hebrews 12:1)

Let's talk about it.

Regarding Hebrews 12:1, how can remembering these witnesses help us in our own journey with Christ?

DAY 56

FREE DAY

[Scheduled Reading: Free/Catch-up Day]

I heard a teacher say that the Bible is half judgment and half mercy.

The Old Testament is full of God's judgment – as well as God's mercy.

In the gospels, Jesus speaks of both mercy ("blessed are those…"); and judgment ("woe to those…").

It's time to turn to Revelation. When most people think of Revelation, they think of curses.

Yes, there's extreme wrath and judgment in Revelation.

There's also extreme mercy in the end.

DAY 57

JESUS' BOOK

[Scheduled Reading: Revelation 1-6]

For eight weeks, our theme has been The Seed.

The Seed of the woman is introduced in Genesis 3:15.

The rest of the Old Testament charts the genealogy of The Seed.

After four thousand (4,000) years and over sixty (60) generations, The SEED finally arrives.

As we enter the New Testament, the gospels present the life and ministry of The SEED.

Finally, we arrive at the last book of the Bible: *The Revelation to John.*

The first five words introduce the book as "The revelation of Jesus Christ."

If you turn to the last page of your Bible, you'll notice the final words of Revelation – "*The grace of the <u>Lord Jesus</u> be with all. Amen.*" (Rev 22:21)

The book of Revelation begins with The SEED... and ends with The SEED.

Often when we think of Revelation, we envision Jesus sitting on the sideline while God works out His wrath and judgment.

But that picture is just not true.

Jesus is the central figure throughout the book. He is the primary agent of wrath and judgment.

As you read the book of Revelation, pay attention to the many references to Jesus (the Lamb, the rider of a white horse, the one seated on the throne, etc.).

And if you have a red-letter print Bible that marks the words of Christ, notice his message to the churches in Chapters 2 & 3.

Remember, Revelation is Jesus' book. It's the Revelation of Jesus Christ.

DAY 58

THE PLAYERS

[Scheduled Reading: Revelation 7-12]

There's a lot in Revelation I don't fully understand.

And if this is one of your first reads through the book, it can be overwhelming.

Here are some helpful rules for newer readers of Revelation:

1. Don't try to understand all the symbolism and deeper meanings of things that are not so clear.

2. Do focus on the things that are clear! (There's plenty to understand).

Also, I find it helpful to stay focused on the key players:

-   Jesus – The SEED. Again, this book is His revelation. He's the central figure, not a sideline spectator.

-   God – Surprisingly, His activity throughout the book appears minimal, but God is directing the entire show.

-   Angels (good guys)

-   Demons (bad guys)

-   The two witnesses (believed to be Elijah and Moses)

-   The Serpent = Dragon = Satan (different descriptions of the same entity)

-   The Beast & the False prophet – (together with Satan, the three make up the unholy trinity)

-   Various multitudes

- Great multitudes who stand before the Lamb

- Various armies (good guys and bad guys)

- Souls beheaded for not taking mark of the beast

- Servants who worship the Lamb in New Jerusalem

- Those inflicted by various plague & judgments

- The dead (those names not in the Lamb's Book of Life).

Every person or creature - holy or unholy - has a future.

Each has an eternal state destined for them according to the prophecies in this book.

DAY 59

THE FALL OF BABYLON

[Scheduled Reading: Revelation 13-18]

The eventual "crushing" the enemy will happen in stages.

Before the final judgment of the dead (those names not in the book of life), Satan is thrown into the eternal lake of fire (Chapter 20).

And before Satan's demise, the False Prophet (anti-Christ) and the Beast will be cast into this fiery lake (Chapter 19).

And before that, we have the "Fall of Babylon" (Chapter 18).

So what and where exactly is this place Babylon?

Throughout scriptures, Babylon is a symbol for godlessness.

Whenever God calls out evil and gives it a figurative reference, He typically mentions "Babylon."

Ancient Babylon was situated in the Mesopotamian region.

It is believe the Garden or Eden was located near ancient Babylon. Satan's entrance on to the scenes of scriptures might have occurred near what later became ancient Babylon.

God's hatred and wrath against Babylon is well documented. Ancient Babylon was a highly cultural and political mecca with flourishing arts, commerce and ideas… and rampant worship of a host of gods.

Centuries after the flood, Babylon suffered God's judgment for its "Tower of Babel" experiment. God dispersed its inhabitants across the earth to slow down their progressive ways (i.e. a tower toward the heavens).

It's no wonder that centuries later God would lead Abram's family away from Ur (near Babylon) to a new land of Canaan.

God was intentional in moving the future of the Seed Family away from Babylon.

And for an ironic twist - to demonstrate God's extreme wrath and judgment on Israel for their sins - where did He send them into exile?

Answer: To Babylon!

In Revelation, an angel from heaven describes "Babylon the Great" as a "dwelling place for demons" (18:2).

Babylon appears to be the dwelling place of remaining expressions of evil and wickedness in these near-end times.

As in the past, it makes sense that this Babylon will exist as a worldwide commercial epicenter. Chapter 18 suggests Babylon's downfall will be accomplished, in part, by the collapse of it's economic empire.

From God's perspective, judgment is not just limited to people or creatures. God's curse is inflicted on "places" as well (cities, regions, etc.).

The final defeat of Satan (remember Genesis 3:15, the crushing blow to the serpent's head) is preceded by a death blow to Satan's preferred place of business... Babylon!

Day 60

COMING SOON

[Scheduled Reading: Revelation 19-22]

Several years ago during my first *Power Read* attempt (a 30-day journey), I read the book of Revelation in a single sitting.

The book hit me like a freight train - jolting my spiritual senses, reminding me how serious God's plan really is.

As I mentioned earlier, I don't have to understand all the symbolism and eschatological events to benefit from the read.

There's plenty to understand in plain English.

Yes, it's dark...dreary...frightening... and sad.

But in Jesus' view, the wrath and judgment is just... and it's coming! (Soon, by the way.)

After 20 chapters of dreadful judgment, death, blood, battles, plagues, etc. - we finally come to the end (which is really the beginning).

After death and hades (that's hell) are swallowed up in the lake of fire, the new heaven and new earth appear (chapter 21).

We get the dimensions of the New Jerusalem (that's going to be like heaven's capital city).

We get a blueprint of the city and it's precious materials - streets of gold, gates made of giant pearls. And there's the tree of life again (remember the Garden of Eden?).

Kings from the earth will bring their splendor into the gates. (Pretty cool).

Be sure to note the final Chapter 22.

Three times, Jesus says *His* return will be soon (verses 7, 12, 20). Jesus is coming to reward those whose names are in the book of life (v12).

Do you remember where we started with this journey (in Genesis 3:15)?

A seed from the woman will one day crush The Seed of the enemy.

We're still waiting for these final events to unfold.

Just as so many earlier prophecies have been fulfilled, we can trust these final events will come to pass as well.

And there's a special blessing in store for those who read and keep the words of the prophecy of this book (v.7). All the more reason to make sure we read this book regularly.

Lets review one more time

The Bible is about the Journey of The Seed

- that travels through 4,000 years,

- consisting of roughly 60+ generations,

- connected by six (6) key reset events,

- focused on two (2) resurrection events,

- which set up one (1) climactic redemptive event: the recreation of the Heavens and the Earth.

CONGRATULATIONS! YOU'VE DONE IT.

But what's next for your journey?

Friends,

It's been an awesome privilege to walk these sixty days with you. I hope this reading journey has been a blessing to you and that you'll continue to make Bible reading a part of your life.

I love hearing about your reading, or group-facilitating experiences, so feel free to drop me a note at www.JeffAndersonAuthor.com.

While you're there, subscribe to my newsletter for more resources and updates.

Thank you!

Jeff Anderson

TIMELINE
CALCULATIONS

TIMELINE CALCULATIONS

Using the verse references, calculate the age and date of each father in the Timeline of The Seed.

Answers are on the next pages.

Timeline from Adam to Flood

Seed	Reference	Age when son born	Date
1. Adam	Gen 5:3	*130*	*4004 BC**
2. Seth	Gen 5:6	*105*	*3874 BC*
3. Enos	Gen 5:9		
4. Cainan	Gen 5:12		
5. Mahalaleel	Gen 5:15		
6. Jared	Gen 5:18		
7. Enoch	Gen 5:21		
8. Methuselah	Gen 5:25		
9. Lamech	Gen 5:28		
10. Noah	Gen 5:32, 11:10		
The Flood	Gen 7:6		
Years from Adam to Flood			

*Starting Date taken from the work of Archbishop James Ussher's Chronology from *Annals of the World*

Timeline from Flood to Abraham

Seed	Reference	Age when son born	Date
11. Shem	Gen 11:10	*2**	
12. Arphaxad	Gen 11:12		
13. Salah	Gen 11:14		
14. Eber	Gen 11:16		
15. Peleg	Gen 11:18		
16. Reu	Gen 11:20		
17. Serug	Gen 11:22		
18. Nahor	Gen 11:24		
19. Terah	Gen 11:26		
20. Abraham			
Yrs from Flood to Abraham			

* Shem had his son 2 years after the flood

TIMELINE CALCULATIONS: ANSWERS

Timeline from Adam to Flood

Seed	Reference	Age when son born	Date
1. Adam	Gen 5:3	130	4004 BC*
2. Seth	Gen 5:6	105	3874 BC
3. Enos	Gen 5:9	90	3769 BC
4. Cainan	Gen 5:12	70	3679 BC
5. Mahalaleel	Gen 5:15	65	3609 BC
6. Jared	Gen 5:18	162	3544 BC
7. Enoch	Gen 5:21	65	3382 BC
8. Methuselah	Gen 5:25	187	3317 BC
9. Lamech	Gen 5:28	182	3130 BC
10. Noah	Gen 5:32, 11:10	500	2948 BC
The Flood	Gen 7:6	100	2348 BC
Years from Adam to Flood		1,656 yrs	

*Starting Date taken from the work of Archbishop James Ussher's Chronology from *Annals of the World*]

Timeline from Flood to Abraham

Seed	Reference	Age when son born	Date
11. Shem	Gen 11:10	2*	2346 BC
12. Arphaxad	Gen 11:12	35	2311 BC
13. Salah	Gen 11:14	30	2281 BC
14. Eber	Gen 11:16	34	2247 BC
15. Peleg	Gen 11:18	30	2217 BC
16. Reu	Gen 11:20	32	2185 BC
17. Serug	Gen 11:22	30	2155 BC
18. Nahor	Gen 11:24	29	2126 BC
19. Terah	Gen 11:26	70	2056 BC
20. Abraham		0	
Yrs from Flood to Abraham		292 yrs	

* Shem had his son 2 years after the flood

Share Power Reading

If you're interested in having me speak at your event, or want to host this 60-Day Power Read experience at your church, please contact us.

We have free facilitator guides and videos for your church and group.

www.PowerReadTheBible.com/Resources/

and

www.JeffAndersonAuthor.com

The results of the 60-Day Bible Read Experience in the lives of our people was life-changing. The living and active Word of God, coupled with Jeff's guidance through its pages, is a powerful force! —Pastor Eric Bryan, Fellowship Bible Church

ABOUT JEFF ANDERSON

Jeff Anderson speaks and writes about walking with God with an approach that combines scripture and story. He's the author of several books, *Plastic Donuts* and *Divine Applause* (Mult-nomah/Random House), *Power Read the Bible,* and *An Advent Journey.* Jeff and his wife, Stephanie, have four children.

www.JeffAndersonAuthor.com

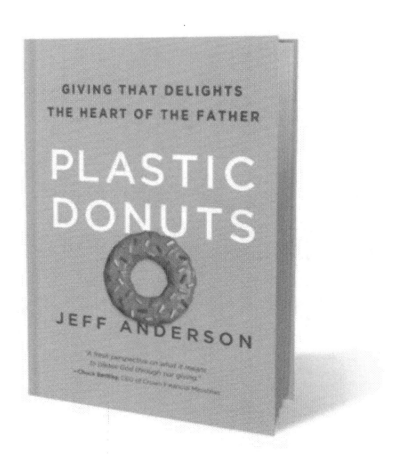

PLASTIC DONUTS IS THE STORY OF A SPECIAL GIFT THAT HELPED ME TO SEE GIVING FROM GOD'S PERSPECTIVE.

Instead of bringing us closer to God, and each other, the topic of financial giving is murky for most believers.

This is why I wrote *Plastic Donuts*.

The message is the result of my deep-dive study of roughly 2,000 gift mentions in the Bible. *Plastic Donuts* takes away the awkwardness that so often accompanies the subject of giving, and replaces it with biblical clarity.

Contact us about free group-study resources, sermon notes, and campaign materials.

Jeff Anderson is a longtime friend. He is highly qualified to share the principles and practices of generosity with others because he personally lives them. Want to become more generous? Learn how from Acceptable Gift.
—Chuck Bentley, CEO, Crown Financial Ministries

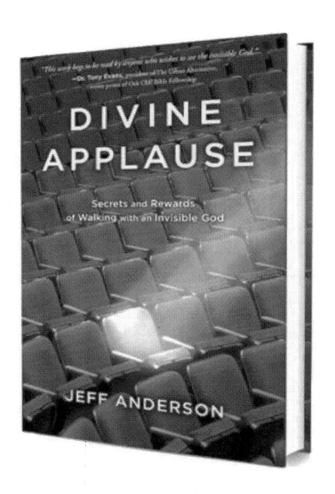

"This study begs to be read by anyone who wishes to see the invisible God."
—Dr. Tony Evans, president of The Urban Alternative,
senior pastor of Oak Cliff Bible Fellowship

DIVINE APPLAUSE

Secrets and Rewards
of Walking with an Invisible God

JEFF ANDERSON

HOW DO WE HAVE A RELATIONSHIP WITH A GOD WE CAN'T SEE?

It's tough being separate from God, and even tougher because we don't know what we're missing. We can't hear His voice or see the Fatherly love in His eyes.

Or can we?

- Experience God's attention in unmistakable ways
- Cultivate an awareness of God's presence
- Enjoy the reward of secrets between you and God
- Take risks to break out of a status-quo life and connect more personally with God
- Discover how God is intensely interested in *you*

You don't have to settle for a distant relationship with God.

God is invisible. At last we have a book that addresses this reality in a creative, refreshing, and encouraging manner.

—Dr. Richard Blackaby, author of *Unlimiting God,*
co-author, *Experiencing God*

This work begs to be read by anyone who wishes to see the invisible God.

—Dr. Tony Evans, President, The Urban Alternative.

Senior Pastor, Oak Cliff Bible Fellowship

ARE YOU INTERESTED IN READING THE ENTIRE BIBLE, COVER TO COVER?

What if I told you that you could read it in 60 days? Seriously.

For many years, I've been helping people to "Power Read the Bible" in just two months.

People really do want to read the Bible. And most important-ly, they want to understand it.

The Power Read the Bible journey will help you to see that the Bible is *readable* and *understandable,* especially when read quickly.

There's something else that helps people achieve their Bible read-ing goals – encouragement.

For 60 days I'll help you keep the Bible's big picture in view by providing daily insights and encouragement to help you stay on track.

Make this the year you finally read through the entire Bible. And I'll help you do it in 60 days!

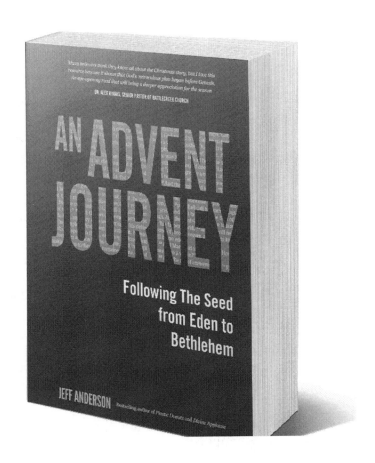

AN ADVENT JOURNEY

Following The Seed from Eden to Bethlehem

You and your family can discover the big picture of the Bible through this eye-opening, daily reading.

In just five minutes per day, discover the real story behind the Christmas story.

Made in the USA
San Bernardino, CA
28 January 2020

63668284R00095